CALIFORNIA FIFTH EDITION

# HOW TO
# CHANGE
# YOUR NAME

BY ATTORNEYS DAVID VENTURA LOEB & DAVID W. BROWN

EDITED BY LISA GOLDOFTAS

NOLO PRESS          BERKELEY

## YOUR RESPONSIBILITY WHEN USING A SELF-HELP LAW BOOK

We've done our best to give you useful and accurate information in this book. But laws and procedures change frequently and are subject to differing interpretations. If you want legal advice backed by a guarantee, see a lawyer. If you use this book, it's your responsibility to make sure that the facts and general advice contained in it are applicable to your situation.

## KEEPING UP-TO-DATE

To keep its books up to date, Nolo Press issues new printings and new editions periodically. New printings reflect minor legal changes and technical corrections. New editions contain major legal changes, major text additions or major reorganizations. To find out if a later printing or edition of any Nolo book is available, call Nolo Press at (510) 549-1976 or check the catalog in the *Nolo News,* our quarterly newspaper.

To stay current, follow the "Update" service in the *Nolo News.* You can get the paper free by sending us the registration card in the back of the book. In another effort to help you use Nolo's latest materials, we offer a 25% discount off the purchase of any new Nolo book if you turn in any earlier printing or edition. (See the "Recycle Offer" in the back of the book.)

This book was last revised in: **March 1994.**

|                |                  |
|----------------|------------------|
| FIFTH EDITION  |                  |
| Third Printing | March 1994       |
| EDITOR         | Lisa Goldoftas   |
| COVER DESIGN   | Toni Ihara       |
| BOOK DESIGN    | Terri Hearsh     |
| ILLUSTRATIONS  | Mari Stein       |
| INDEX          | Sayre Van Young  |
| PRINTING       | Delta Lithograph |

Loeb, David V.
How to change your name / by David Ventura Loeb & David W. Brown;
edited by Lisa Goldoftas. -- California 5th ed.
                     p. cm.
ISBN 0-87337-125-9 : $19.95
1. Names, Personal--Law and legislation--California. I. Brown;
David Wayne II. Goldoftas, Lisa III. Title.
KFC109.L6 1990
346.794'01'2--dc20
[347.9406121]

## DEDICATION

This book is dedicated to its original author, David Ventura Loeb.

## ACKNOWLEDGMENTS

Thanks to the many people who helped bring this book into being: Ken Twisselman, Suzanne Marychild, Ed Sherman, Trudy Ahlstrom, Mary-Lynne Fisher and David Loeb's friends: Nora, David and Darrell.

Special thanks to everyone whose time and expertise added to this edition: Jake Warner, for his fine eye and tireless queries; Stephanie Harolde, for preparing copies of the manuscript; Terri Hearsh, for turning straw into gold in the production of this book; Jackie Mancuso, for her design expertise; Toni Ihara, for creating yet another beautiful cover; David Freund, for reviewing forms and proofreading; and everyone else at Nolo whose hard work and enthusiasm add to every book.

# CONTENTS

IF YOU WANT TO CHANGE your name but are reluctant—or unable—to pay several hundred dollars for an attorney, this book is for you. *How to Change Your Name* gives information about different methods of going about a name change. It provides all the forms and instructions you'll need to legally change your name in California.

Every year, thousands of Californians officially change their names. The number is growing as people realize that there's no reason to be stuck with a name they don't like. For example, one Californian petitioned to change his name from Steamboat Robert E. Lee Green Leaf Strong Boy of the Wind to Robert Di Brezzio.

*How to Change Your Name* covers name changes in these and similar situations:

- **Name Changes After Marriage, Divorce or Annulment:** A woman may legally keep her birth name when she marries or revert back to her birth or former name after using her husband's name. A husband and wife can change their last names to a combination of the two or something altogether different. A divorced woman still using the last name of her "ex" can easily change back to a former name.
- **Name Changes for Unmarried Couples:** A couple need not be legally married to assume the same last name. For example, some lesbian and gay couples choose to use the same last name as part of their commitment to one another. The name may be the last name of one of the members of the couple, a hyphenated combination of the names or an altogether different name.
- **Children's Names:** Often a divorced parent with sole custody of the children wants to change their names. Sometimes legal guardians prefer a child to have their last name. Other times, mature children have a

preference for a certain name. This book gives guidance on when and how these changes can be accomplished.

- **Immigrant Names:** Maybe an ancestor changed his name from Finkelstein to Ford when he came to the United States in the 1880's. As people rediscover their heritages, changing last names back to their original ancestral names is common. Of course, there is also the reverse situation—for someone who feels no connection with a heavy six-syllable name, keeping it makes little sense.
- **Lifestyle and Convenience:** Why be called Rudolph, Marguerite or Penelope when you feel that Glenn, Jennifer or MaryAnn better expresses the real you? One friend of mine who was tired of being last in every line changed his last name from Zywik to Aaron.
- **Religious and Political Names:** Some people may wish to change their names to reflect their religious or political beliefs. Some famous political and religious leaders have taken on new names, such as Mother Teresa and Malcolm X.

Let your imagination wander for a moment and consider what name you would have chosen for yourself. Your name may be crucial to your self-image and how you feel about yourself. For those who want to make a change, this book will take you through the process. It's easy.

Icons are used throughout this book to alert you to information specifically directed to:

women    married couples    children

## TWO WAYS TO CHANGE YOUR NAME

IN CALIFORNIA, ADULTS (people over age eighteen) have always had the right to use the first, middle and last names of their choice. Once a name change is accomplished in California, the new name is valid everywhere. There are two legally valid and acceptable ways to change a name in this state:

- Usage; and
- Court Petition.

### Other Ways to Change Your Name

Upon request from a woman obtaining a divorce or annulment in California, a judge must restore her birth or former name, even if a request was not included in the petition (Family Code §§2080, 2081). Obtaining a name change that way is cheaper and more convenient than other available methods. (See Chapter 3, Sections B, C and D.)

Sometimes a birth certificate may be changed to reflect a new name. If a change is accomplished this way, no Court Petition is needed. (Detailed information about birth certificates is covered in Chapter 5.)

## A. USAGE METHOD

YESTERDAY, YOU WERE Irving Worms. Today, tomorrow and for the rest of your life, you can be David de la Rouge. How? Just by using the new name consistently. A name change by the Usage method is accomplished by simply using a new name in all aspects of your personal, social and business life. No court action is necessary, it costs nothing and is legally valid (Code of Civil Procedure §1279.5).[1]

The key requirement to this method is *consistency*. You must use the same name with everyone, all the time. Someone who uses a new name in only one part of his life has not legally changed his name. For example, an actor who uses a new stage name only in his profession has not changed his name.

**Note:** If you decide to change your name by the Usage method, read and follow the instructions in Chapters 7 and 8.

## B. COURT PETITION METHOD

A NAME CHANGE BY Court Petition is accomplished by completing a few forms and filing them with the court. Then a short notice stating that you are changing your name must be published in a local newspaper. Unless someone objects, your name change will normally be

---

[1] A number of California court cases have affirmed an adult's "common law" right to a name change without going to court (*Lee v. Ventura County Superior Court* (1992) 9 Cal. App. 4th 510, 513, 11 Cal. Rptr. 2d 763; *Cabrera v. McMullen* (1988) 204 Cal. App. 3d 1; *In re Ritchie* (1984) 159 Cal. App. 3d 1070; *In re Banks Marriage* (1974) 42 Cal. App. 3d 631; *Sousa v. Freitas* (1970) 10 Cal. App. 3d 660; *Application of Trower* (1968) 260 Cal. App. 2d 75).

approved without even a court hearing. [2] Occa-sionally, a brief appearance before a judge is required. If so, the procedure is not difficult to handle on your own following the instructions in this book.

The cost to do your own name by Court Petition is $182 for court filing fees, plus about $40 to $200 for publication fees. Actual costs depend on the county and newspaper—and court fees may be waived altogether if you have a very low income. If you hired an attorney, you'd expect to spend an additional several hundred dollars or more to undertake a procedure you can easily and safely do yourself with the help of this book.

## C. WHICH METHOD SHOULD YOU CHOOSE?

PEOPLE UNDER AGE EIGHTEEN cannot have their names legally changed by the Usage method. Their names must be changed by the Court Petition method. [3]

If you are over eighteen years old, you are considered an adult in California, and have a choice between the Usage or Court Petition method. A name change by Usage is just as legal as a Court Petition change, and costs nothing. A name change by Court Petition will cost some money and will take a small amount of your time. Of course, both methods require that you let others know that you have changed your name.

So why use the Court Petition method if it costs more? Practically speaking, an official court document makes it much easier to get everyone to accept your new name. Because many people and agencies do not know that a Usage name change is legal, they may want to see something in writing that was signed by a judge. Also, certain types of identification—such as a passport and birth certificate attachment reflecting the new name—are not readily available to those who change their names by the Usage method. (See Chapter 8.)

For some people, the act of going to court and getting a name change is an important process. Like other legal proceedings, such as a divorce, there may be a personal need to obtain an official resolution. It also may be important to some people to have the name change a matter of public record.

But it's also possible that you have personal reasons for keeping your name change relatively private. In that case, changing your name by Usage will allow you to take on a new name without creating a public court record or pub-lishing notice of the proposed change in a local newspaper.

If you decide not to go through the court, you may have small hassles with people who don't believe a name change is legal without a court order. You may want to just try the Usage method and see how it goes. If you run into barriers, you can always file a court petition later.

---

[2] If you are a parent petitioning for the name change of a minor child, the other parent must be formally notified of the proposed name change. (This is covered in detail in Chapter 6, Section J.)

[3] Sometimes a minor's name can be changed by having a new birth certificate issued. See Chapter 5, Section A.

# CHAPTER 2

## RESTRICTIONS ON NEW NAMES

ONE LEGAL DEFINITION OF a person's name is "the distinctive characterization in *words* by which he is known and distinguished from others."[1] Most new names of choice fall within the bounds of that description, but occasionally they present a problem.

If you change your name by Court Petition, the judge can refuse to grant a new name if a substantial reason exists for the denial. The limitations on choosing a new name are:

- You may not choose a name with "fraudulent purposes"—meaning you intend to do something illegal. For example, you may not legally change your name if your reason is to avoid paying debts, to keep from getting sued or to get away with a crime.
- You may not "interfere with the rights of others," which generally means capitalizing on the name of some famous person.
- You may not use a name that would be "intentionally confusing." This might be a number or punctuation (e.g., "10" or "?").
- You may not choose a name that is a racial slur.
- You may not choose a name that could be considered a "fighting word," which includes threatening or obscene words, or other words likely to incite violence.

---

[1] *Putnam v. Bessom* (1935) 291 Mass. 217, emphasis added.

**Note:** Obviously, if you change your name by Usage, there's no opportunity for someone to formally object. If someone doesn't want you to use a certain name, he would have to contact you personally or file a lawsuit to prevent you from using the name. Practically speaking, if you use the Usage method to change your name to one that a judge wouldn't grant, you're likely to have problems getting your new name accepted.

## A. FAMOUS NAMES

FAMOUS PEOPLE, SUCH AS celebrities, politicians and other public figures, do not have monopolies on their names. For example, if you look in telephone directories of most large cities, you'll find listings for John Wayne, Elizabeth Taylor, Gerald Ford and Michael Jackson.

You can generally assume the name of a famous person as long as:
- You're not adopting the name with fraudulent purposes;
- You wouldn't likely be confused with the famous person, which might be the case if you live nearby or have a similar profession;
- You will not benefit commercially or economically by using the name; and
- Your use of the name will not cast the famous person in a negative light.

Some years ago, an aspiring actor with an exceptional talent for impersonating a famous movie star petitioned the court to have his name changed to Peter Lorie. The court refused the petition when the real Peter Lorre objected to the name change.[2]

In another case, a California resident petitioned a Los Angeles court to change his name to Jesus Christ, and the name change was granted. Perhaps in an effort to stall for time, the court clerk made a diligent attempt to determine if the name change was fraudulent. He found a Jesus Witness Christ living in East Los Angeles, and a Jesus J. Christ in Santa Monica. It turns out that Christ is a not-uncommon German last name and Jesus is a common Hispanic name, and there seemed to be no showing of fraud.

**Note:** Some famous names belong to people who have died. In California, their heirs have a legal right to prevent you from using the name for purposes of economic gain (Civil Code §990). By filing a special document with the state, the heirs may preserve the right to a name for 50 years.[3]

## B. PROFESSIONAL AND FICTITIOUS NAMES

FICTITIOUS NAMES, SUCH AS those used by movie characters or companies, could be protected by copyright, trademark or corporate law. If you plan to use such a name to make money or promote yourself or a product, you run the risk of a legal battle. You could try to get advance consent from the person or company with rights to the name, but it's not likely you'd get it. However, if you simply want to use a fictitious name for personal reasons, you probably won't have problems. Or you might consider modifying the name so it's similar, but not identical, to the well-known fictitious name.

Movie stars often have a glamorous stage name for the theatre marquee, while in their daily affairs they use their original names. After all, Norma Jean Baker does not sound as special as Marilyn Monroe. Likewise, some writers have a "nom de plume." It is perfectly legal to use a professional name in addition to your everyday name as long as you are not doing it for fraudulent purposes. Adopting a second name does not accomplish a name change. Your original name remains as your legal name for official records unless you use the new name in all aspects of your life.

Women who have become established in their professions before marriage often continue to use their birth names professionally, even when they adopt their husband's last name for all other purposes. Although this sometimes creates confusion, it is legally acceptable. (See Chapter 3 for more information on married women and names.)

## C. INITIALS, NUMBERS AND ONE-WORD NAMES

AN INITIAL IS LEGALLY sufficient as a first, middle or last name. The initial does not have to stand for a longer name. One example of a well-known person who used an initial for a last name is Malcolm X. The "S" in former president Harry S Truman's middle name never stood for anything—the letter was his middle name.

A court may use its discretion in refusing a name change to a number. For example, Thomas Ritchie III failed in his court petition to change his entire name to the Roman numeral "III," apparently because the judge determined that a Roman numeral is simply not a name and was

---

[2] *In re Weingand* (1964) 231 Cal. App. 2d 289, 41 Cal. Rptr. 778.

[3] Only a handful of states have similar laws. Case law concerning these matters is frequently contradictory. If you want to take on the name of someone famous who is still living or who died within the last 50 years, you could face legal action if you use the name for commercial or economic gain.

inherently confusing (*In re Ritchie* (1984) 159 Cal.App.3d 1070, 206 Cal.Rptr. 239).[4]

California law does not specify whether you can change your name to just one word (like "Moonbeam" or "Freedom").[5] However, individual judges have granted name changes to just one name. Since the main purpose of a name is to identify you, one name should be acceptable if this purpose is satisfied. After all, many people have name-alikes which are only distinguishable by their address and social security number.

The State Registrar of Vital Statistics will accept a birth certificate which contains only a last name. A contract signed with your one name is considered a valid contract. You can get a driver's license in your "full true name," whatever that may be. The Registrar of Voters reports that they have registered people who changed their names by Court Petition to just one name ("especially rock stars").

Practically, you will run into problems if you only use one name. Every form you fill out demands at least two names, and computers have trouble fathoming single name people. You'll also likely run into resistance from fussy bureaucrats. If you want to try using one name and it becomes too much trouble, you can always adopt a single initial for your first or last name.

## D. RACIAL SLURS, "FIGHTING WORDS" AND OTHER FORBIDDEN NAMES

YOU MAY NOT USE the Court Petition method to change your name to one which includes a racial slur or other words that offend others so intensely that they are likely to respond with violence. An African-American educator from Thousand Oaks attempted to change his name to "Misteri Nigger" (pronounced "Mr. Nigger"). Although his motive was a good one, namely "to steal the stinging degradation—the thunder— from the word nigger," and thus "to conquer racial hatred," the court ruled that a racial epithet, i.e., a disparaging or abusive word which may be a "fighting word," may not be adopted by the Court Petition method.[6] So, regardless of your intentions in choosing a new name, a court may deny it if it is an ethnic slur or includes words of threat or profanity.

But can you change your name to something like Crack Cocaine or Merri Christmas? That depends on the judge, who has discretion when deciding whether to grant a name change. "Crack Cocaine," for example, might be denied in today's political climate. But what about "Merri Christmas?" There's a good chance that a judge would grant it. In fact, it's been done.

---

[4]Minnesota's Supreme Court ruled that a man who wanted to change his name to the one number "1069" could not legally do so, but suggested that "Ten Sixty-Nine" might be acceptable (*Application of Dengler* (1979) 287 NW2d 637).

[5]Other states' courts have approved name changes to one-word names. In the Missouri case of *In re Reed* (1979) 584 SW2d 103, an appeals court reversed a trial court's refusal to grant Morris Edward Reed's requested change of name to "Sunshine," and ordered the trial court to grant the request.

[6]*Lee v. Ventura County Superior Court* (1992) 9 Cal. App. 4th 510, 11 Cal. Rptr. 2d 763.

## E. MISS, MRS., MS., MR. OR MASTER

YOU ARE ALLOWED TO use whatever title or form of address you choose, regardless of age or marital status, as long as there is no intent to defraud anyone. For example, a married woman may use Miss as well as Mrs. or Ms., if she chooses. Increasingly, people aren't using any title—but if used, it is not considered part of a legal name.

It's possible a judge would deny your name change request if you wanted to change your first name to a title. It might be considered inherently confusing, especially if you wanted to adopt the title of the opposite gender.

*It is of chief importance, in the law of change of name*
*that by Usage or court method, it is legal all the same.*
*If the name by which you're called now is not the proper sort,*
*despite all that they've told you, you needn't go to court.*
*Of a new name the requirement, which won't cost you a dime, is to use*
*the name exclusively, and that means all the time.*

*But alas, there is a limit on the name that you can use—*
*you don't have total freedom your newfound name to choose.*
*The courts have now decided you cannot use the name*
*of certain well-known persons who have acquired fame.*
*You cannot choose a name for purposes of fraud,*
*nor can you pick a number, not an even or an odd.*

*Neither do you have court petition right*
*to use a name that will cause a fight.*
*And while a court can grant a name that's inane,*
*it probably won't let you have one that's profane.*
*Your new name may properly confound the census,*
*but cannot extremely offend the senses.*

*A woman getting married, on our part of the earth,*
*may through continued usage retain her name of birth.*
*And whether married or divorced, legality won't lack*
*for women with their husband's names to take their birth names back.*
*In summary, the name by which you've wanted to be known*
*may instantly be taken, and now used as your own.*

—Dave Brown

# CHAPTER 3

## MARRIAGE, DIVORCE, ANNULMENT AND NAMES

THE MOST COMMON QUESTION women used to ask concerning names was whether a married woman must adopt her husband's last name. Of course, the answer is "no." A woman may choose to take on her husband's last name, keep her former name or adopt a totally different one. A woman may also decide to change her name a number of times. For example, a woman might take her husband's last name when she marries, resume her birth name[1] when she divorces, and change to her new husband's last name when she remarries.

Some women feel that even a birth name is only an expression of a paternal heritage and decide to take on a totally different name. For example, some women add the word "child" to their mother's first name and use this as a last name—such as Suzanne Marychild. These new names may be adopted by using either the Usage or Court Petition method.

---

[1]Until recent years, a woman's birth name was always referred to as her "maiden name." In 1974, the California legislature changed "maiden" name to "birth" name in some of the more important laws dealing with names. The term "birth" name is used in this book.

### Women's Names and Credit

By law, a woman cannot be discriminated against in businesses or credit matters because of her choice of name. California law requires that all businesses accept a married woman's birth or former name if she regularly uses it, regardless of her marital status (Code of Civil Procedure §1279.6). Credit card companies must issue credit cards in a woman's birth or married name—the choice of name is entirely up to her. However, the credit card company may insist that a married woman establish an account separate from her husband's (Civil Code §1747.81).

## A. MARRIAGE AND NAMES

PEOPLE WHO MARRY ARE free to keep their own names, adopt either last name for use by both, hyphenate their names, or choose a completely new name. For example, you and your husband may want to both be known by a hyphenated combination of your last names (Him-Her). Or you could pick an altogether different last name that resembles neither name.

Over time, whatever name you use after marriage will appear in more and more records—such as your driver's license, taxes and credit cards. You can save yourself considerable time and trouble by making sure you are happy with your choice of name before any records are changed. Many women wish they had never adopted their husband's last name, but after years of usage feel that it's too much trouble to re-adopt their old one.

California courts have upheld the right of women to retain or return to their birth or a former name by either the Usage or Court Petition method. Lower courts have routinely granted married women's petitions to return to their birth names, and are required to allow this in divorce cases, even long after the divorce is final. (See Section B, below.) In analogous court cases, it has been held that a married woman may be sued in her birth name, and a wife's last name does not automatically change when her husband changes his unless she consents.[2]

### Who Are You This Time?

It's not uncommon for women who are or have been married to go by different names. Often, some official records are changed to a married name while others are left in the birth name.

Women who don't consistently use the same name are bound to run into occasional confusion and inconvenience. For example, a woman who has a bank account in her birth name may need to supply a copy of her marriage license to the bank before she is allowed to cash checks payable to her in her married name.

Some agencies and institutions will insist on seeing official identification or documentation before they will change their records.

## 1.  Returning to Birth or Former Name While Married

A married women who has been using her husband's last name may choose to change back to a birth or former name. Although the decision for such a name change commonly is a mutual decision between both members of the couple, the husband's consent is not needed.

People may confuse your name change with a divorce or remarriage, so you may run into some hassles even though the process is the same as any other name change. Since you legally changed your name to that of your husband when you got married, you must now reverse the process. Either the Usage or Court Petition method may be used.

If you change your name by Court Petition, it's extremely rare that a judge will want to know if your husband agrees with the change. It's not required for your husband to co-sign the petition or attend the hearing in the unusual case where a court hearing is necessary—but he could do so.

**Note:** You can use the Declaration Restoring Former Legal Name set out in Chapter 7, Section B if you change your name by the Usage method.

---

[2]*Sousa v. Freitas* (1970) 10 Cal.App.3d 660, 89 Cal.Rptr. 485.

## 2. Keeping Your Name When You Marry

There is no law in California that requires a woman to assume her husband's name upon marriage—and today many choose not to. But it is also common for a woman to take on her husband's last name when she marries. Simply by following the Usage method of name change, her husband's last name becomes her new legal name. In this commonly accepted situation, there is little hassle getting people to accept the new name because this type of name change is customary.[3] In fact, the change is often made with a smile and maybe even a "congratulations."

If you want to keep your name when you marry, simply don't change it. There's no need to file any documents with the court, since a married woman acquires her husband's name only by Usage anyway. Just don't start using your husband's name, and keep your own name on all records.

As a matter of common sense, you shouldn't go around notifying agencies and businesses that you got married but don't want your records changed. You will only risk confusing people. It's possible, of course, that some of your records may even get changed to your husband's name when the news of your marriage filters through the bureaucracy. If so, you will have to contact someone about changing those records back. (See Chapter 8.)

### A Word About "Lucy Stoners"

Over the years, many woman have chosen to keep their birth names. Lucy Stone began the tradition in 1855, when she created a furor as the first American woman to keep her name after marriage.

From her example, the Lucy Stone League was founded in New York in 1921 by Ruth Hale, a New York journalist. Hale kept her own name after marrying Heywood Broun in 1917, and was a purist when it came to her name. Reportedly, as she was coming back down the aisle after her wedding, a well wisher hoping to be the first to call her by her new name, said "Hello, Mrs. Heywood Broun." Hale snapped back, "I am not Mrs. Heywood Broun. I am Ruth Hale. Don't ever call me Mrs. Broun." If people phoned her at home and asked for Mrs. Broun, she would say, "Mrs. Broun does not live here," and then curtly give them the phone number of her husband's mother. Invitations addressed to Mr. and Mrs. Broun meant that she was not invited. Only her pet cat was properly called Mrs. Heywood Broun.

"A married woman who claims her own name is issuing a challenge…It is a defiance, and as such is dealt with by society, under a hundred euphemisms, always with hostility." These words of Ruth Hale, written in the early part of the century, still merit attention.

A "Lucy Stoner" became the dictionary definition of "a person who advocates the keeping of their own names by married women." Some of the early Lucy Stoners included Amelia Earhart, Edna St. Vincent Millay and Margaret Mead.

---

[3]Some businesses may insist on seeing a copy of the marriage certificate before they will change their records. If so, remind them that is illegal under Code of Civil Procedure Section 1279.6.

## a. Marriage Surname Agreement (Antenuptial Agreement)

If you want to keep your own name after marriage, you will probably want to discuss your decision with your fiancé. It's possible that you may even want to formalize your plans with a written agreement. While not required, a written agreement may be a reminder that you chose to retain your name for positive reasons, should years dim the memory of your discussion. It also may help convince a government or business bureaucrat that you have legitimately elected to keep your birth or former name.

The Marriage Surname Agreement (Antenuptial Agreement) provided in Appendix 1 specifies that the woman intends to keep her former or birth name when she marries. "Antenuptial" simply means "before marriage." An antenuptial agreement is a legal contract between two people who are planning to get married. Use the accompanying sample as a guide to complete the agreement.

---

### MARRIAGE SURNAME AGREEMENT
#### (Antenuptial Agreement)

This agreement is made between _____ [woman's name] _____

and _____ [man's name] _____ in consideration of

the contemplated marriage of said parties.

It is hereby agreed between the parties that _____ [woman's name] _____

upon and during the marriage will not assume the surname of _____ [man's last name] _____,

but will retain her own name.

NOTICE IS HEREBY GIVEN to all agencies of the State of California, all agencies of the Federal

Government, all creditors and all private persons, groups, businesses, corporations and associations, that

_____ [woman's name] _____ will retain for all purposes said name upon

and during her marriage to _____ [man's name] _____.


Dated: _____         _____

                                                        (signature)

Dated: _____         _____

                                                        (signature)

## B. DIVORCE AND NAMES

A WOMAN OFTEN CHANGES her name at the time of divorce. She may want to return to a birth name, a name from a previous marriage or some other name she has used.[4] If there are children, the name change isn't affected by who has custody or what last name the children have.

If the divorce takes place in California, the judge must make a formal order restoring your birth or former name if you request it (Family Code §§ 2080, 2081). This may be done in the petition, at the court hearing or after the divorce is final. (See Section D, below, for instructions.)

If she wants, a woman may keep her husband's last name, and can even go by the first and last name of her ex-husband (for example, Mrs. Robert Myex). The only exception would be to use the name fraudulently. For example, you cannot use an ex-husband's name in order to falsely pass yourself off as still married or to avoid creditors.

## C. ANNULMENT AND NAMES

WOMEN WHOSE MARRIAGES have been annulled have the legal right to return to their former or birth name (Family Code §2080). The request may be made in a petition, at the time of hearing or after judgment. Follow the procedure in Section D just below.

---

[4]There seems to be no legal authority allowing a man to get a court order to return to his former name as part of a divorce action in situations where he has adopted a hyphenated name or a completely new name at the time of the marriage. However, a man in this situation may as well ask the court to make the change and see what happens. At worst, he will be told that he has to file a separate court action to change his name—unless, of course, he wants to follow the Usage method, which is always available.

## D. HOW TO CHANGE A NAME AFTER DIVORCE OR ANNULMENT

YOU CAN ALWAYS CHANGE your name by the Usage Method. You may wish to use the Declaration Restoring Former Legal Name provided in Chapter 7, Section B. Or you may choose not to prepare any name change documents; because women often return to their former names after divorcing, the Usage method usually goes smoothly.

If your marriage was dissolved or annulled by a court, it's possible the judge ordered that your name be changed in the process. Check the final order that was signed by a judge. If the court ordered your name be changed to the name you want, the order is all the paperwork you'll need. You may want to get certified copies of the order as proof of the name change; check with the court for details.

If you want to change your married name to your birth name or a former name, there's an easy way to do it if the divorce or annulment took place in California. You need only fill out a straightforward and simple one-page Ex Parte Application for Restoration of Former Name After Entry of Judgment and Order form. (A sample follows and a blank copy of this form is included in Appendix 2 at the back of the book.) Make sure you use the correct caption and case number from the divorce or annulment case. There's no need to send a copy of the Application to your former spouse. File the Application with the Court in which the divorce or annulment was filed and pay the filing fee of about $14. After the judge signs the form, a certified copy is your proof that your former legal name has been restored.

If you want to change your name to anything other than a birth name or former name, you may use either the Usage method or Court Petition method.

| ATTORNEY OR PARTY WITHOUT ATTORNEY *(Name and Address)*: | TELEPHONE NO.: | FOR COURT USE ONLY |
|---|---|---|

ATTORNEY FOR *(Name)*:

**SUPERIOR COURT OF CALIFORNIA, COUNTY OF**

STREET ADDRESS:

MAILING ADDRESS:

CITY AND ZIP CODE:

BRANCH NAME:

**MARRIAGE OF**

PETITIONER:

RESPONDENT:

| EX PARTE APPLICATION FOR RESTORATION OF FORMER NAME AFTER ENTRY OF JUDGMENT AND ORDER | CASE NUMBER: |
|---|---|

## APPLICATION

1. A judgment of dissolution or nullity was entered on *(date)*:

2. Applicant now requests that her former name be restored. Her former name is *(specify)*:

Date:

..............................................................
(TYPE OR PRINT NAME)                                    ►                    (SIGNATURE OF APPLICANT)

## ORDER

3. IT IS ORDERED that applicant's former name is restored to *(specify)*:

Date:

_____
☐ JUDGE OF THE SUPERIOR COURT   ☐ COMMISSIONER OF THE SUPERIOR COURT

---

[SEAL]

### CLERK'S CERTIFICATE

I certify that the foregoing is a true and correct copy of the original on file in my office.

Date:                    Clerk, by _____ , Deputy

| Form Adopted by Rule 1287.50 Judicial Council of California 1287.50 [New January 1, 1987] | EX PARTE APPLICATION FOR RESTORATION OF FORMER NAME AFTER ENTRY OF JUDGMENT AND ORDER (Family Law) | Civil Code, §§ 4362, 4457 |
|---|---|---|

# CHAPTER 4

## CHILDREN'S NAMES

IT IS INCREASINGLY COMMON for parents and children to have different last names due to divorce, remarriage or a mother retaining her birth name. Parents sometimes have questions about what names their children legally may go by and how a name change can be accomplished.

## A. NAMES YOU MAY GIVE A CHILD AT BIRTH

IN THIS COUNTRY, it is common for children to take their father's last name, but it is not required by law.[1] Customs differ in other places. In many Spanish-speaking countries, a child's last name is a combination of the mother's and father's last names. In medieval France, a common practice was for girls to take their mother's last name and boys to take their father's last name.

In California, you can legally give your children any last name you wish, including:

- The mother's last name;
- The father's last name;
- A combination of both last names (for example, Duffey-Loeb); or
- A last name that is totally unrelated to either of the parents. For example, Jane Fonda and Tom Hayden named their son Troy O'Donovan Garity.

When naming a child, you should not choose a name with "fraudulent purposes," a name that "interferes with the rights of others," or a name that would be "intentionally confusing." (See Chapter 2 for more information on limitations of names.)

You should never give a child the last name of a man who is not the true father because you think it will get him to assume responsibility. That will not make him legally responsible for the child, and it will be difficult later to get names changed on the birth certificate.

When your child is born in a hospital, you give a hospital worker information that will go on the child's birth certificate. Before you sign the completed birth certificate, make sure the child has the name you've chosen. Don't be intimidated into using the father's last name if you have decided on another.

---

[1]In California, the father does not have an absolute right to give the child his surname if the mother objects. The sole consideration is "the best interests of the child." (See *In re Marriage of Schiffman* (1980) 28 Cal. 3d 640, 169 Cal. Rptr 918; *Donna J. v. Evna M.-W.* (1978) 81 Cal. App. 3d 929.)

### 1. Parental Agreement on Child's Name

Although not necessary, it is a good idea for both parents to sign a simple written agreement if they decide to give a newborn child a different last name from the father. For both married and unmarried couples, whether lesbian, gay or hetersexual, this can help avoid confusion, both when the original birth certificate is filled out and possibly later, should the parents separate.[2] A Parental Agreement on Child's Name is provided in Appendix 1.

## B. CUSTODY, REMARRIAGE AND CHILDREN'S NAMES

GIVING A CHILD A DIFFERENT NAME from the father or changing the child's name does not change the child's "paternity" (legally-recognized identity of the real father). It also does not affect the rights or duties of either parent regarding visitation, child support or rights of inheritance.

[2]Information about children born to unmarried couples, as well as forms for acknowledging parenthood are contained in two Nolo Press books: *The Living Together Kit* by Toni Ihara and Ralph Warner and *A Legal Guide for Lesbian and Gay Couples* by Hayden Curry and Denis Clifford.

This change only occurs if the father's identity is established in a court hearing or the child is legally adopted.

One potential area of conflict is where there is a divorce and the mother gets custody of the children. Then she remarries and wants the children of her former husband to bear the name of her new husband. Or she changes back to her former name and wants her children's names changed to match.

Traditionally, courts ruled that a father had an automatic right to have the child keep his last name if he continued to actively perform his parental role. No longer.[3] Now a child's name may be changed by court petition when it is in the best interest of the child to do so. When deciding whether to grant a name change, courts consider the length of time the father's name has been used, the strength of the mother-child relationship and the need of the child to identify with the new family unit through use of a common name. Overall, the courts must balance these factors against the importance of the father-child relationship. What this all boils down to is that it's up to a judge to decide which name is in the child's best interest.

## C. NAMES, PATERNITY AND BIRTH CERTIFICATES

ONCE A PERSON IS LISTED on a birth certificate as a father, it is often impossible to get his name removed, even if the mother later states that he is not the father. Giving the child the name of a man and saying that he is the father doesn't make it so. It's a lousy idea to give a child the name of a man who is not the father and to list that person as the father on the birth certificate.[4]

[3]*Marriage of Schiffman* (1980) 28 Cal. 3d 640, 169 Cal. Rptr 918.

[4]Lesbian couples who both wish to be listed as parents may be able to do so. See Chapter 5.

## PARENTAL AGREEMENT ON CHILD'S NAME

This agreement is made between _____ and
_____ in consideration of the contemplated birth
of a child born of said couple.

It is hereby agreed between the parties that the child will be given the _____
name of _____.


Dated: _____        _____
(signature)

Dated: _____        _____
(signature)

Unless a man was married to and living with a child's mother when the child was conceived, he can always claim that he is not the father. If he does this, he has a right to a court hearing. This could result in his being found not to be the father at the same time that his name is on—and will stay on—the birth certificate.

Sometimes a child's name can be changed on a birth certificate without the need for a court order. Other times, the birth certificate can be changed following a court paternity action. If the child's name is changed on a birth certificate, a legal name change is accomplished. No court order is required. (For more details about when and how a child's name can be changed on a birth certificate, see Chapter 5.)

*I have no name*
*I am but two days old.*
*What shall I call thee?*
*I happy am*
*Joy is my name,*
*Sweet Joy befall thee!*

*Pretty joy!*
*Sweet joy but two days old,*
*Sweet joy I call thee:*
*Thou dost smile.*
*I sing the while.*
*Sweet joy befall thee.*

—William Blake, 1789

## D. HOW TO CHANGE A CHILD'S NAME

UNLIKE AN ADULT, whose name can be changed by either the Usage or Court Petition method, a minor's name can normally only be changed by

Court Petition.[5] As long as both parents agree to the change, the court should grant the request automatically. (Step-by-step instructions for changing a name by Court Petition method are contained in Chapter 6.)

A name change petition may be filed by one or both parents. If a parent is seeking a name change at the same time, it may be done in a single petition, unless disallowed by a court's local rules. When one parent files a petition for a child's name change, the other parent must usually be given advance notice of the proposed name change. If you are a woman with custody of children from a prior marriage and you have remarried, your new husband cannot petition to change your children's names unless he has legally adopted them.

If both parents are dead, the petition may be filed by the court-appointed legal guardian, if there is one.[6] Or, if the parent-child relationship is terminated in a legal proceeding, a name change may be included in that process (Family Code § 7638). Otherwise it may be filed by an adult relative or close friend.

Adopted children usually have their names changed as part of the original adoption order. If for some reason this did not occur, the adoptive parents may file a petition on their adopted child's behalf.[7]

---

[5]When a new birth certificate is issued bearing a child's new name, there is no need to go to court for a name change. See Section C above and Chapter 5.

[6]You may be able to obtain a legal guardianship of a minor using *The Guardianship Book: How to Become a Child's Guardian in California* by Lisa Goldoftas and David Brown (Nolo Press).

[7]Special rules exist for a minor age 12 or older who has been relinquished to an adoption agency by his parents but has not been legally adopted. The petition is to be signed by both the minor and the adoption agency. Names and addresses of close relatives do not have to be included in the petition unless the minor knows them.

# CHAPTER 5

## BIRTH CERTIFICATES AND NAMES

A BIRTH CERTIFICATE IS a document used to officially record the birth of a child. Birth certificates provide such information as the child's name, the names of the child's parents and when and where the birth took place. Birth certificates are usually completed by hospital personnel or the person delivering a baby. The State Registrar of Vital Statistics keeps original birth certificates after they have been reviewed by the local health department. Copies are maintained in each county by the local county recorder.[1]

It is not necessary to have a birth certificate changed in order to accomplish a legal name change. In fact, as explained in this chapter, it is very difficult to change a birth certificate, and a legal name change will not get you the right to a new birth certificate.[2] However, if you change your name by Court Petition, an official attachment showing the new name can be added to an original birth certificate (Health and Safety Code §10470).

**Note:** This chapter only covers birth certificates for people born in California. If you were born in another state or country, contact that vital statistics department.

### California Birth Certificates and Same-Sex Parents

Until 1993, the Department of Vital Statistics refused to issue birth certificates listing two same-sex parents. This presented a problem for lesbians who conceived children through artificial insemination and wanted to list the lover as the other parent. Lesbian and gay couples who adopted children were faced with a similar problem.

Beginning in 1993, two same-sex parents may be listed on a California birth certificate. The birth certificate form may be altered to read "mother/parent" for male couples or "father/parent" for female couples. The form is slated to change sometime in the future.

---

[1]Local health departments generally keep copies of birth certificates for the last year or two.

[2]The one exception is where a person born in California has undergone a sex change operation and obtained a court order for a change of name and issuance of new birth certificate. (See Section C in this chapter.)

## A.   WHEN NEW BIRTH CERTIFICATE CAN BE ISSUED

THERE ARE SEVERAL CIRCUMSTANCES listed below where you can get a totally new birth certificate issued if you (or a minor child) were born in California. If one of these circumstances applies, a legal name change can be accomplished simply by getting a new birth certificate and using the new name listed on the new birth certificate— with no need for a Court Petition. If a completely new birth certificate is issued, the old one is sealed and no one can look at it without first obtaining a court order.

The proper application forms for any of the situations discussed in this section are available by mail from the State Registrar of Vital Statistics, Department of Health Services, 304 "S" Street, P.O. Box 730241, Sacramento, CA 95814-0241, Telephone (916) 445-2684. The cost for changing a birth certificate or obtaining a new one is currently $19.00.

### 1.   Acknowledgment of Paternity

Sometimes a birth certificate does not list a child's father. Other times the father is listed, but the child's last name is different from the father's. In these situations, an entirely new birth certificate may be issued (Health and Safety Code §10455). Regardless of whether the child's natural parents were married at the time of birth, later marry, or never marry, missing information about the parent(s) may be added. The child's name may be changed to reflect the father's last name.

The mother and father acknowledging paternity both must be willing to sign statements under penalty of perjury confirming that they are the natural parents and requesting changes to the birth certificate. The form used by the State Registrar of Vital Statistics is "Application for Preparation of an Amended Birth Record After Acknowledgment of Paternity." To follow this procedure, there cannot be conflicting information on the birth certificate. *If a different father*

*was listed on the original certificate, this method will not work.* (See Section A2 of this chapter.)

*Example 1:* Karen Klone and Sam Same have a child named Brad. On his birth certificate, no father is listed and Brad is given a last name Karen made up on the spur of the moment. Karen and Sam file statements acknowledging that Sam is the father and requesting that Sam be listed on the birth certificate. They also ask that Brad be given his father's last name. A new birth certificate is issued showing Sam Same as the father, and Brad Same as the child.

*Example 2:* Rose Red and Omar Orange have a daughter. She is listed on the birth certificate as Shelley Red, with Rose listed as the mother and Omar listed as the father. Rose and Omar file statements requesting that Shelley's last name be changed to that of her father. A new birth certificate is issued listing Shelley Orange as the child.

*Example 3:* Becky Bright and Don Dark have a child before they are married. The child's name is listed on the birth certificate as Tommy Dark, but no father is shown on the birth certificate. After Becky and Don marry, they file statements acknowledging that Don is their child's father. A new birth certificate is issued listing Don Dark as Tommy Dark's father.

## 2.  Judicial Decree of Paternity (Court Order)

A "paternity action" is a court suit filed to have a man declared to be the father of a child. The lawsuit is usually brought by the father, mother or district attorney. Many paternity actions are initiated by district attorneys on behalf of county welfare offices that provide financial assistance to families and are required by law to seek reimbursement from the father. When a man is legally deemed to be the father, he has a duty to support the child. His visitation rights and the child's rights to inherit are also affected.

If the court finds that a certain man is the father, it issues an order stating this fact, often referred to as a "judicial decree of paternity" or "adjudication of paternity." Once a judicial degree of paternity is obtained in California or another state, a new California birth certificate may be issued (Health and Safety Code §10450). Information about the father may be included, and the child's last name may be changed to that of the father. If another man was listed as the father on the original birth certificate, that information is not shown on the new one.

## 3.  Adoption (Court Order)

In legal adoptions, a new birth certificate is issued if requested.[3] Adopted children usually have their names changed as part of the original adoption order. The court clerk is responsible for sending notice of the adoption to the State Registrar of Vital Statistics no later than five days after the adoption is finalized. If the adopting parents wish, a new birth certificate can be issued for the child exclusively in the name of the new parents (Health and Safety Code §10430).

## 4.  Sex Change Operation (Court Order)

People born in California who have undergone a surgical sex change operation may obtain a new birth certificate in the new name and gender. They must first go to court and obtain an order that affirms both the gender and new name. Then a form must be completed and filed with the State Registrar of Vital Statistics, along with the appropriate fee—currently $19.00. (See Section C below.)

## 5.  Offensive Racial Description

While not a name change, a new birth certificate may be issued if it contains a derogatory, demeaning or colloquial racial description. To have the birth certificate changed, you must identify the term you want changed, provide an accurate racial description and pay a specified fee—currently $19.00 (Health and Safety Code §10406). Contact the State Registrar of Vital Statistics to obtain the necessary forms.

---

[3]Stepparents can handle their own adoptions using *How to Adopt Your Stepchild* by Frank Zagone and Mary Randolph (Nolo Press).

## B. ADDING AMENDMENT TO BIRTH CERTIFICATE

SOMETIMES YOU ARE NOT eligible to obtain a completely new birth certificate, but you may be entitled to have an official attachment added to the birth certificate. The special amendment is physically attached to your birth certificate and becomes an official part of that record. However, it does not actually change the birth certificate. Application forms for the situations discussed in this section are available from the State Registrar of Vital Statistics, Department of Health Services, 304 "S" Street, P.O. Box 730241, Sacramento, CA 95814-0241, Telephone (916) 445-2684. Some forms are also available from local county recorders. Check in the county listing in the government section of the phone book, and call for details.

### 1. Adding New Name After Court Order Name Change

If you were born in California and your name is changed by a court order, you may arrange for an official attachment to be added to your birth certificate. The court order may be issued by a court in California or any other state or territory of the United States (Health and Safety Code §10470). To arrange for an official attachment to your birth certificate, you'll need to complete Form VS (Vital Statistics)-23, an "Application for Amendment of Birth Record to Reflect Court Order Change of Name." The State Registrar of Vital Statistics' filing fee is currently $19.00.

### 2. Errors and Missing Information on Birth Certificate

Occasionally, errors are made on original birth certificates. Typically these are typographical errors—for example, listing "Nose" instead of "Rose" for a child's name. Sometimes an item is left blank—such as a child's first or middle name. Or perhaps a child is accidentally listed as the wrong sex. Most substantial changes, such as

completely changing a listed first name—for example, changing "Mary" to "Phyllis"—will not be accepted unless you can come up with a very good explanation to show that it really was an error at the time the certificate was filled out.

Errors on original birth certificates may be corrected by physically attaching a special amendment to a birth certificate and making it an official part of that record (Health and Safety Code §10400). However, the birth certificate itself is not changed. To correct an error, you must complete a form and submit it to the State Registrar of Vital Statistics. The form requires that two people sign affidavits—statements signed under penalty of perjury. One affidavit is usually completed by one of the child's parents. The other affidavit can be from the other parent or anyone who knows about the error. If an incorrect gender is listed and the birth was recent, a hospital official should complete an affidavit whenever possible.

There is no charge for correcting errors to a birth certificate if the change is made within one year of a child's birth. The State Registrar of Vital Statistics' fee is currently $19.00 if the change is made after one year. Depending on the circumstances, the correct form would be either "Application to Amend a Record" or "Application to Complete Name of Child by Supplemental Name Report—Birth."

*If the wrong father was listed on the birth certificate, this method cannot be used to correct either the certificate or the child's last name, regardless of the explanation.* (See Sections A1 and A2 in this chapter.)

### 3. Adding Parent's New Name to Child's Birth Certificate

After a parent's name is changed by Usage or Court Petition, an attachment showing the parent's new name may be added to the child's birth certificate. The attachment indicates that the parent is "AKA" (also known as) and gives the new name. Adding an attachment will not change the child's name and it will not result in a new birth certificate being issued.

The form used to reflect a parent's use of an additional name is "Application to Amend a Record." The form requires that two people sign affidavits—statements signed under penalty of perjury. The filing fee is currently $19.00.

*If the wrong father was listed on the birth certificate, this method cannot be used to correct either the certificate or the child's last name, regardless of the explanation.* (See Sections A1 and A2 in this chapter.)

**Note:** Although an attachment may be added to the child's birth certificate showing a parent's Usage name change, the parent cannot add such an attachment to her own birth certificate unless she changes her name by Court Petition.

## C.  OBTAINING NEW BIRTH CERTIFICATE AFTER SEX CHANGE OPERATION

PEOPLE UNDERGOING SEX CHANGE operations have special considerations when it comes to name changes. They can change their names by either the Usage or Court Petition method. Some prefer to change names by the Usage method in order to keep the matter out of public record. Others choose to be publicly open about the change to obtain a court order they can show to agencies and others who might otherwise question the change.

Until a surgical sex change operation is complete, a name change does not legally accomplish a change in gender. For example, even if the name on a driver's license is changed from a masculine-sounding name to a feminine-sounding one, the gender listed on that license does not change. However, the gender may be changed on a California driver's license once sex change surgery is complete. To do this, the doctor who performed the surgery must fill in forms which are then filed with the Department of Motor Vehicles.

But what about that birth certificate that says "Mary" instead of "Mark," and reflects the old gender? Since 1977, people born in California who have undergone sex alteration surgery may obtain a new birth certificate if they file a petition with the court (Health and Safety Code §§10475-10479). They must then send a request to the State Registrar of Vital Statistics and pay a filing fee. The old birth certificate is sealed and can only be opened with a court order.

Unfortunately, people born outside of California will be limited to a Court Petition name change only. They must check with the authorities in their state of birth to see whether a birth certificate in a new gender can be obtained there. (Good luck.)

Here's how to change your name and obtain a new birth certificate. Prepare and file documents for a change of name and issuance of new birth certificate following the instructions below. With the payment of a single court filing fee, you can get an order changing both your name and gender. Once a judge signs the order, contact the State Registrar of Vital Statistics and have a new birth certificate issued.

The procedure, following completion of a sex-change operation, for changing one's name and legal gender by Court Petition method is summarized below.

## 1. Change Name By Court Petition Method

Follow the instructions for changing your name by the Court Petition method set out in Chapter 6 with the following exceptions. Complete the required forms substituting the following instructions for corresponding items. Note that you may need to squeeze some words in, or white-out and retype sentences in the forms. Make sure you obtain at least three certified copies of the decree.

### a. Petition for Change of Name

**Caption:** After the title "PETITION FOR CHANGE OF NAME," add the words "AND ISSUANCE OF NEW BIRTH CERTIFICATE (Health and Safety Code Section 10477)."

**Item 1:** Fit in "and issuance of new birth certificate" after the words "why this application for change of name." After listing your present name and proposed new name, add the words, "and that this court make an order for the issuance by the State Registrar of Vital Statistics, pursuant to Section 10477 of the Health and Safety Code, of a new birth certificate reflecting applicant's proposed name as *(new name)* and sexual gender as *(male/female)*."

**Item 6:** You must list California as the state of birth. Otherwise, you will be limited to a name change petition only.

**Item 7:** Fill in: "Applicant has undergone surgical treatment for the purpose of altering Applicant's sexual characteristics to those of the opposite sex. A declaration or affidavit of *(name of M.D. certifying sex change operation)*, M.D., a physician duly licensed to practice in this state, documenting this alteration surgery, is attached as Attachment 7 and incorporated by reference."

You must then get a signed declaration by a licensed California medical doctor stating that the sex change surgery has taken place and specifying the new sexual gender. The statement must end with: "I declare under penalty of perjury under the laws of the State of California that the foregoing is true and correct." The doctor must date the declaration as well as sign it. (For a sample of a declaration, see Chapter 6, Section J3b.)

### b. Order to Show Cause for Change of Name

**Caption:** After the title "ORDER TO SHOW CAUSE FOR CHANGE OF NAME," add the words "AND ISSUANCE OF NEW BIRTH CERTIFICATE."

**Item 1:** After the words "Petition for Change of Name," fit in "and issuance of new birth certificate." After listing your present and proposed new names, add the words, "and that this court make an order for the issuance by the State Registrar of Vital Statistics, pursuant to Section 10477 of the Health and Safety Code, of a new birth certificate reflecting applicant's proposed name as *(new name)* and sexual gender as *(male/female)*."

**Item 2:** After the words, "application for change of name," fit in "and issuance of new birth certificate."

### c. Decree Changing Name

**Caption:** After the words "DECREE CHANGING NAME" add "AND ORDER FOR ISSUANCE OF NEW BIRTH CERTIFICATE."

**Item 1:** After the words "Petition for Change of Name," fit in "and issuance of new birth certificate." After listing your present and proposed names, add the words, "and for an order for the issuance by the State Registrar of Vital Statistics, pursuant to Section 10477 of the Health and Safety Code, of a new birth certificate reflecting applicant's proposed name as *(new name)* and sexual gender as *(male/female)*."

**Item 3:** After listing your present and proposed new names, add the words, "and that the State Registrar of Vital Statistics issue a new birth certificate reflecting Applicant's name as *(new name)* and sexual gender as *(male/female)*."

## 2. Obtain New Birth Certificate

Contact the State Registrar of Vital Statistics, Department of Health Services, 304 "S" Street, P.O. Box 730241, Sacramento, CA 95814-0241, telephone (916) 445-2684. Request the appropriate form to change your name and gender on your birth certificate. You'll need to send a certified copy of the Decree Changing Name along with a completed form and appropriate fee (currently $19.00). A copy of the new birth certificate will be sent to you.

**CHAPTER 6**

## COURT PETITION METHOD

IT DOESN'T TAKE A LAWYER to do a perfectly acceptable name change by the Court Petition method. People sometimes think lawyers have special knowledge that an average person cannot understand. In truth, many routine legal matters can easily be understood and accomplished by you. Handling your own name change can be an eye-opening experience in self-sufficiency.

## A. OVERVIEW OF PROCEDURE

IN THIS CHAPTER ARE step-by-step instructions for changing your name by the Court Petition method.[1] Here's an overview of what's involved:

1. Complete several fill-in-the-blanks forms:
   - Petition for Change of Name;
   - Order to Show Cause for Change of Name; and
   - Decree Changing Name.
2. File your papers with the county clerk, get a court date and pay a filing fee. (If you have a very low income, you'll need to complete two short documents to obtain a fee waiver.)
3. If you are changing the name of a minor, both living parents must know about the petition. If only one parent signs the petition, the other parent must personally receive papers about the name change proceeding.[2] If both parents are dead, the petition may be filed by a legal guardian or adult relative.
4. Arrange to have notice of the name change published once a week for four consecutive weeks in a newspaper you have selected. After publication has been completed, make sure that the newspaper files an Affidavit of Publication with the court.
5. Check with the court to see if an objection has been filed and whether a court hearing is required. If no hearing was scheduled—which is common in many courts—obtain two

certified copies of the Decree Changing Name which was signed by the judge. If a hearing is required, go to court at the assigned time and present your point of view to the judge.
6. Send a certified copy of the Decree Changing Name to the California Secretary of State.
7. Notify agencies and business about your name change following the guidelines in Chapter 8.

## B. INFORMATION ABOUT COURT AND FORMS

THE FORMS REQUIRED FOR a name change are easier to complete than most job applications. Filling out forms can be fun, especially when you realize that otherwise you would pay a lawyer hundreds of dollars to do it for you.

### 1. Call Superior Court Clerk

Name change petitions are filed in the Superior Court of the county in which the person seeking a name change lives. Some of the larger counties have branch courts in several cities. If there is a branch court close to where you live, you'll probably need to file your papers there. The front white pages of the telephone book has a government section. Call the number listed for the Superior Court in your county and say that you are filing a name change petition and would like to know:

- The proper branch of the court for filing your papers. Tell the clerk in what city or town you (or the minor for whom you are seeking a name change) live.
- Mailing address of the court.
- Street address of the court—if it is different from the mailing address.
- Filing fee for filing a name change petition. (If you cannot afford the fees, you may be able to get them waived. See Section G2 in this chapter.)
- Whether only local forms must be used (see "Local Forms" below.

---

[1]If you are also seeking a change in gender following a sex change operation, see Chapter 5, Section C.

[2]You may request a waiver of the service requirement following the instructions in this chapter.

- Whether local printed instructions for name changes are available. Some courts give information about specific local rules, form preparation, service of process and attendance at hearings.

### Local Forms

There are no standardized forms used throughout California for name changes. Some Superior Courts have promulgated forms for this purpose, and sell them for a small fee or distribute them without charge. Other courts are familiar with forms put out by companies in the area, such as the California Newspaper Service Bureau.

Some courts are flexible about which forms they'll accept, while others may be resistant to filing unfamiliar forms. If your court will only accept local forms, you'll find the instructions in this chapter can easily be adapted to suit those particular forms.

### 2.  Tips on Completing Forms

Before you get started, here is some basic information you'll need to know about filling in forms. If you follow these suggestions, you can save a lot of time and trouble.

- Before you fill out any of the tear-out forms provided in the Appendix at the back of this book, make several photocopies of each. This will save you many worried moments if you make a mistake or misplace a form. Also, note that some forms have printing on both sides. You can copy each side on a separate piece of paper and staple the pages together before filing the form with the court, or you can make two-sided copies.
- All forms should be completed carefully and neatly, preferably using a typewriter. It is best to use the larger type size (called "pica" or "10-pitch" type). Some courts may refuse to accept forms with smaller type (called "elite" or "12-pitch" type). If you do not have access to a typewriter, the court may provide one for

public use, or a local library may rent them. [3] (In many places, there are typing and paralegal services which can prepare forms for you at a reasonable cost. See Chapter 9, Section A.)

- Carefully follow the instructions in this book for completing the forms. Also look at the samples provided to make sure you fill them in correctly.

---

[3]Depending on the court's policies, handwritten forms may be accepted if you print clearly and neatly, generally in black ink. If you want to submit handwritten forms, call the filing clerk beforehand to make sure they'll be accepted.

| PARTY WITHOUT AN ATTORNEY ( *Name and Address*):    TELEPHONE NO.: | FOR COURT USE ONLY |
|---|---|
| *In Pro Per* | |

**SUPERIOR COURT OF CALIFORNIA, COUNTY OF:**

STREET ADDRESS:

MAILING ADDRESS:

CITY AND ZIP CODE:

BRANCH NAME:

IN THE MATTER OF THE APPLICATION OF:

| **PETITION FOR CHANGE OF NAME** | CASE NUMBER: |
|---|---|

### 3.   How to Complete the Caption

Most forms follow a standard, fill-in-the blanks format. The first page of each form has a heading of several boxes with blank spaces, which is referred to as a "caption." The caption is filled in the same way on every form. Here is how to do it.

**Party Without Attorney:** Fill in your present name in capital letters, followed by your mailing address and telephone number. "In Pro Per" means you are acting as your own attorney.

**Name of Court:** In capital letters, fill in the county in which you are filing your papers.

**Court Address:** In the spaces provided, fill in the court's street address, mailing address, and city and zip code. Also fill in the branch name, if there is one.

**In the Matter of the Application of (Name):** In capital letters, fill in the *present* full first, middle and last names of each person who wants his name changed. Do not fill in any new proposed names, even if you've started using them. Make sure that all names are consistent, complete and correctly spelled. Do not use nicknames or initials unless they are meant to be in place of a name.

**Form Title:** Each form has a title, such as "Petition for Change of Name" or "Order to Show Cause for Change of Name." The title does not have to be altered.

**Case Number:** Leave this space blank, since you don't have a case number yet. When you file your papers with the court, you will be assigned a case number which will be stamped or written on the papers. (If you later need to file additional papers, carefully copy the case number from papers previously filed with the court.)

## Terms Used in Name Change Forms
## (Who's Who and What's What)

To complete the court forms required for a name change, you'll need to know these essential terms. They are used throughout the instructions.

**Applicant:** The person whose name is to be changed. There may be more than one Applicant in one petition—for example, a mother and a child. When the Applicant is under age 18, list the minor's name and the words "a minor" (for example, "Kevin Apple, a minor").

**Petitioner:** The person(s) completing the forms and requesting the name change. This is usually also the Applicant, unless she is a minor.

**Present Name:** The complete old name you want to change. Even if you have already been using the new name by the Usage method, your old name is referred to as the "present" name.

**Proposed Name:** The complete new name by which you want to be known.

## C. SELECT NEWSPAPER FOR PUBLICATION

A NAME CHANGE WILL GIVE you the chance to get your name in the newspaper—at least, in the "Legal Notices" section next to the want ads. You'll need to have several paragraphs of information published in a newspaper once a week for four weeks. Almost any daily or weekly newspaper of general circulation that is printed in your county is acceptable, as long as the newspaper has been certified as a "newspaper of general circulation" by the Superior Court for that county.[4]  If they run legal ads, they're certified. Even small weekly newspapers can qualify to be so certified, and their publication rates tend to be significantly lower than regular daily newspapers.

---

[4]If there is no newspaper published in your county, the clerk of the court may post the order in three of the most public places in the county (Code of Civil Procedure §1277). That process is explained in Section I of this chapter.

To find newspapers in your county, get a recommendation from the court clerk or local law library or look in the yellow pages under "Newspapers." Call the newspapers and find their rates for publishing an Order to Show Cause for Change of Name once a week for four weeks. Rates may vary drastically from newspaper to newspaper, and you can save yourself some money by checking around. For example, we recently found publication rates ranging from $40 to $200 in the same county.

When you've selected the newspaper, make sure you get the full, correct name of that paper. For example, if you plan to use the "San Francisco Banner Daily Journal," you'd need to use that full name, not the "SF Banner."

## D. PETITION FOR CHANGE OF NAME

THE PETITION FOR CHANGE of Name gives the basic facts the judge needs to grant your name change. A single petition can be used for more than one person—such as a couple or parent and children.

| PARTY WITHOUT AN ATTORNEY (*Name and Address*): | TELEPHONE NO.: | FOR COURT USE ONLY |
|---|---|---|
| KRISTOPHOS YUKABONKERZKAPOWPOLIS<br>20 Anystreet<br>San Jose, CA 95110          (916) 555-1212<br><br>*In Pro Per* | | |

**SUPERIOR COURT OF CALIFORNIA, COUNTY OF:**  SANTA CLARA
STREET ADDRESS: 191 North First Street
MAILING ADDRESS:
CITY AND ZIP CODE: San Jose, CA 95113
BRANCH NAME:

IN THE MATTER OF THE APPLICATION OF:
KRISTOPHOS YUKABONKERZKAPOWPOLIS and JANE
YUKABONKERZKAPOWPOLIS, a minor

| **PETITION FOR CHANGE OF NAME** | CASE NUMBER: |
|---|---|

1. Petitioner(s) ___KRISTOPHOS YUKABONKERZKAPOWPOLIS___

    request(s) that this court make an order to show cause at a specified time and place why this application for change of name should not be granted, and upon hearing this court make an order changing Applicant(s)' name from
    KRISTOPHOS YUKABONKERZKAPOWPOLIS to KRIS KAPOW
    _and from JANE YUKABONKERZKAPOWPOLIS_
    to _JANE HELEN KAPOW_

2. ☒  There are two or more Applicants. The information requested in Items 3-10 for each additional Applicant is supplied in a separate Attachment 2.

3. Applicant *(name)*: ___KRISTOPHOS YUKABONKERZKAPOWPOLIS___

    a. ☒  was born on ___January 1___, 19_50___ and is over the age of eighteen years.

    b. ☐  is a minor under eighteen years of age, born on _____, 19_____, and is related to the Petitioner(s) as: _____.

4. Applicant's present name is: ___KRISTOPHOS YUKABONKERZKAPOWPOLIS___.

5. Applicant's proposed name is: ___KRIS KAPOW___

6. Applicant was born in ___San Diego, California___, and presently resides at
    ___20 Anystreet, San Jose, CA 95110___, in the County
    of ___Santa Clara___, State of California.

7. The reason for the proposed name change is:

    Petitioner's present name is inconvenient, hard to spell, unappealing, embarrassing and confusing. Petitioner's proposed name better suits his present identity. Therefore Petitioner is known by and wishes to be known by his proposed name in all his social and business affairs.

---

*NP*                          **PETITION FOR CHANGE OF NAME**

| IN THE MATTER OF THE APPLICATION OF: | CASE NUMBER: |
|---|---|
| KRISTOPHOS AND JANE YUKABONKERZKAPOWPOLIS | |

8. ☐ Additional facts supporting petition are as follows:

    a. ☐ Applicant's father consents to the proposed name change.

    b. ☐ Applicant's mother consents to the proposed name change.

    c. ☐ Other:

9. The names, residence addresses and relationships of Applicant's relatives so far as known to Petitioner(s) are as follows:

    a. ☒ Father: ROBERT YUKABONKERZKAPOWPOLIS, deceased

    b. ☒ Mother: ANNA YUKABONKERZKAPOWPOLIS, 3000 51st Avenue, San Francisco, California 94111

    c. ☐ Applicant's father and mother are deceased. Applicant's near relatives, their relationships and respective residence addresses so far as known to Petitioner(s), are as follows:

10. ☐ *(Complete only if Applicant is a minor.)* Petitioner(s) request(s) that notice to the following person(s) be dispensed with for the reasons specified in Attachment 10:

    a. ☐ Applicant's father *(name):* _____

    b. ☐ Applicant's mother *(name):* _____

11. ☒ Number of pages attached:  1

I declare under penalty of perjury under the laws of the State of California that the foregoing is true and correct.

Date: May 2, 19__

_Kristophos Yukabonkerzkapowpolis_
_____          _____
Signature of Petitioner                              Signature of Second Petitioner

KRISTOPHOS YUKABONKERZKAPOWPOLIS
...........................................          ...........................................
(Type or Print Name)                              (Type or Print Name)

NP                          **PETITION FOR CHANGE OF NAME**

---

| IN THE MATTER OF THE APPLICATION OF: KRISTOPHOS AND JANE YUKABONKERZKAPOWPOLIS | CASE NUMBER: |
|---|---|

**ATTACHMENT 2 TO PETITION FOR CHANGE OF NAME: INFORMATION ON ADDITIONAL APPLICANTS**
*(use a separate Attachment for each additional applicant)*

3. Applicant *(name):* __JANE YUKABONKERZKAPOWPOLIS__

   a. ☐ was born on _____, 19____ and is over the age of eighteen years.

   b. ☒ is a minor under eighteen years of age, born on ___July 20___, 19_86_, and is related to the Petitioner(s) as: his daughter

4. Applicant's present name is: ___JANE YUKABONKERZKAPOWPOLIS___

5. Applicant's proposed name is: ___JANE HELEN KAPOW___

6. Applicant was born in ___San Jose, California___, and presently resides at 20 Anystreet, San Jose, CA 95110, in the County of ___Santa Clara___, State of California.

7. The reason for the proposed name change is:

See reasons stated for Petitioner KRISTOPHOS YUKABONKERZKAPOWPOLIS.

Applicant's proposed surname is the same as her father's. It is in the best interests of the Applicant to have the same surname as the Petitioner, preventing embarrassment and inconvenience.

8. ☒ Additional facts supporting petition are as follows:

   a. ☒ Applicant's father consents to the proposed name change.

   b. ☐ Applicant's mother consents to the proposed name change.

   c. ☐ Other:

9. The names, residence addresses and relationships of Applicant's relatives so far as known to Petitioner(s) are as follows:

KRISTOPHOS YUKABONKERZKAPOWPOLIS

   a. ☒ Father: 20 Anystreet, San Jose, CA 95110

   b. ☒ Mother: HELEN YUKABONKERZKAPOWPOLIS, deceased

   c. ☐ Applicant's father and mother are deceased. Applicant's near relatives, their relationships and respective residence addresses so far as known to Petitioner(s), are as follows:

10. ☒ *(Complete only if Applicant is a minor.)* Petitioner(s) request(s) that notice to the following person be dispensed with for the reasons specified ~~in Attachment 10~~ below:

   a. ☐ Applicant's father *(name):* _____

   b. ☒ Applicant's mother *(name):* HELEN YUKABONKERZKAPOWPOLIS is deceased.

---
*NP*     **ATTACHMENT 2 TO PETITION FOR CHANGE OF NAME**

**Caption:** Follow the instructions in Section B3 of this chapter.

**Item 1:** In the first blank, fill in your name, as well as anyone who is petitioning with you. Note that although the Petitioner (person filing documents requesting a name change) and Applicant (person who wants her name changed) are usually the same, they differ when an adult seeks a name change for a minor. An adult seeking a name change for a minor should list her own name rather than minor's name.[5]

In the second set of blanks, fill in the Applicant's present name. After the word "to," fill in the Applicant's proposed name.

**Note:** If you are seeking name changes for more than one Applicant, fill in each of the present and proposed names. Always put the present name first, then the word "to" followed by the proposed name.

**Item 2:** Check this box if you are seeking a name change for more than one person—for example, a family, couple or parent and children. If so, complete Items 3-10 on the petition for only one Applicant. Then you'll need to prepare an attachment page for *each* additional Applicant. Appendix 2 contains the form "Attachment 2 to Petition for Change of Name: Information on Additional Applicants." It is printed in exactly the same format as Items 3-10 of the petition. Simply make a photocopy of Attachment 2 for each additional Applicant. Then complete a separate Attachment 2 for every additional Applicant following the instructions below for Items 3-10.

**Item 3:** Fill in the present name of the Applicant (person whose name is to be changed).

**Item 3a:** Check this box if the Applicant is over eighteen years of age. Then fill in the Applicant's birthdate.

**Item 3b:** Check this box if the Applicant is under eighteen years of age. Then fill in the Applicant's birthdate and specify how the Applicant is related to the Petitioner—for example, son, daughter or ward (a minor with a court-appointed legal guardian).

**Item 4:** Fill in the Applicant's present name. Make sure it is identical to the name listed in the caption of the form.

**Item 5:** Fill in the Applicant's proposed new name. This should be identical to the new name listed in Item 1.

**Item 6:** In the first blank, fill in the Applicant's city and state of birth—including the country if the Applicant was born outside of the United States. In the second blank, fill in the Applicant's complete home address. In the last blank, fill in the California county in which the Applicant presently lives. This must be the same county where you are filing the name change petition, but there is no time requirement for residency—the Applicant might have lived there one week or twenty years.

**Item 7:** Briefly state why you are seeking a name change. The reason doesn't make much difference, since the judge is legally obligated to grant the petition unless there is a good reason to deny it, such as fraud. However, it doesn't look good to only say "Because I've always loved the name Bozo," even if it would get you through.

If the Applicant is already using the proposed name, you have a great reason for the name change request, because one of the purposes of the Court Petition method is to make an official record of Usage name changes. If that is your situation, include the words "is known by" in this item.

Following are some samples. Feel free to vary them and make additions to fit your particular situation. The parts in brackets are alternatives—use them as they apply. Explanations are added in italics where needed. Icons designate when samples typically pertain to women, married couples, or children.

[5]If a minor's parents are living, at least one of them must petition for the name change. If both parents are dead, a legal guardian or adult friend may petition. (See Chapter 4, Section D.)

Petitioner's proposed name is convenient and [he/she] wishes to be known by this name in all [his/her] personal and business affairs.

Petitioner's present name is inconvenient, hard to spell, unappealing, embarrassing and confusing *(use words that apply)*. Petitioner's proposed name better suits [his/her] present identity. Therefore Petitioner [is known by and] wishes to be known by [his/her] proposed name in all [his/her] social and business affairs.

Petitioner's proposed name is an ancestral name. Petitioner [is known by and] wishes to be known by that name in all [his/her] social and business affairs.

Petitioner is known by [his/her] proposed name in [his/her] profession, and wishes to be known by [his/her] professional name in all [his/her] social as well as professional affairs.

*If a couple is changing their last names to a combination of the two:* Petitioner's proposed surname is a combination of [his/her] surname and that of Petitioner's ["lover," "partner" or similar term]. Petitioner [is known by and] wishes to be known by this name in all [his/her] personal and business affairs. ***Note:*** *If you do not wish to make this information part of the public record, simply state: Petitioner's proposed surname is convenient and [he/she] wishes to be known by this name in all [his/her] personal and business affairs.*

Petitioner's proposed name is her birth [or former] name. Petitioner feels her proposed name better suits her present identity and therefore she [is known by and] wishes to be known by her proposed name in all her social and business affairs.
***Note:*** *For women divorced in California, a simple one-page form, Ex Parte Application for Restoration of Former Name after Entry of Judgment, can be filed in the divorce case at a cost of about $14, even years after the divorce was final. In that case, you don't need to use the regular Court Petition method. See Chapter 3, Section B and D.*

Petitioner's marital status is divorced [or widowed]. She [is known by and] wishes to be known by her birth [or former] name in all her social and business affairs.

*If one spouse wants a name change for professional reasons, and both spouses want to adopt the new last name:* Petitioner [husband/ wife] wants to change [his/her] name for professional reasons. Since Petitioners are husband and wife, they wish to be known by the same last name.

*Although you cannot officially change a child's name by the Usage method, be sure to mention if the child is already known by the proposed name:* Applicant's present name is inconvenient, hard to spell, unappealing, embarrassing and confusing *(use words that apply)*. Petitioner prefer Applicant's proposed name. [Applicant is called by his/her proposed name.]

*One or both parents must petition for a name change for a minor unless both parents are dead. Then the petition may be filed by the legal guardian of the minor's person, if there is one. Otherwise, it may be filed by an adult relative or friend.* Applicant's parents are both dead. Applicant has been living in the household of Petitioner since *(give date)*. Petitioner is Applicant's *(specify relationship, such as legal guardian of the person, relative or adult friend)*. It is in the best interests of the Applicant to have the same surname as the Petitioner, preventing embarrassment and inconvenience.

*If a divorced woman with custody of a child wants to change her child's last name, the courts are reluctant to do so without the father's consent. If the father has abandoned his child, the court might grant a name change if the judge thinks it is in the "best interests of the child." Read Section J of this chapter before completing this item:* Petitioner was awarded custody of the Applicant upon her divorce on *(give date)*. The Applicant's natural father has failed to [regularly] make child support payments. [No payments have been received since *(date of last payment)*]. The Applicant's father does not show parental interest in the child and has not [regularly] exercised his visitation rights since *(give date of last visit)*. Petitioner has changed her surname [by remarriage or by returning to her birth or former name]. It is in the Applicant's best interests, preventing embarrassment and inconvenience, to have the same surname as [his/her] mother [and stepfather, half brother, etc.]

Applicant is mature enough to choose [his/her] own name, and wishes to be known by [his/her] proposed name. Petitioner consents to this change of name and also prefers the proposed name.

**Caption for Page Two:** Fill in the name of the Applicant(s). Leave the case number blank since it hasn't been assigned yet.

**Item 8:** Check this box if there are additional facts supporting the name change.

**Item 8a:** Check this box if you are a minor Applicant's father or he agrees with the name change after you discussed the matter with him. (To avoid further hassles, it is best to have both parents sign the petition.)

**Item 8b:** Check this box if you are a minor Applicant's mother or she agrees with the name change after you discussed the matter with her. (To avoid further hassles, it is best to have both parents sign the petition.)

**Item 8c:** Check this box if there are any other facts supporting the name change. While not required, some married women choose to include information about their husband's consent:

Petitioner is married, and her husband agrees with the proposed name change. Petitioner's husband's name is *(name),* and his place of residence is *(street address, city, state).*

**Item 9a:** Check this box and fill in the name and home address of Applicant's father. If he is dead, put the word "deceased" after his name. If you do not know who the father is, fill in "unknown." If you do not know his address, put in the words "address unknown."

**Item 9b:** Check this box and fill in the name and home address of Applicant's mother. If she is dead, put the word "deceased" after her name. If you do not know who the mother is, fill in "unknown." If you do not know her address, put in the words "address unknown."

**Item 9c:** If both of Applicant's parents are dead, check this box. Then fill in the names, relationships and home addresses of known close relatives such as sisters, brothers, aunts, uncles and grandparents. If there is a legal guardian, specify that and include his name and address. If no close relatives are known, type in the words, "As far as known to Petitioner, Applicant has no near relatives."

**Items 10a-b:** Skip this entire item if the Applicant is at least eighteen years old, or the Applicant is under eighteen and both parents sign the petition. If the Applicant is a minor and only one parent signs the petition, the other parent is legally entitled to personally be given documents about the proposed name change. This must be done at least 30 days before the date a judge is scheduled to decide whether to grant the new name.

Sometimes the petitioning parent does not know the whereabouts of the other parent or has a very good reason why the other parent should not be given notice of the proposed name change, such as:

• The father is unknown and is not listed on the child's birth certificate; or

• The other parent has had no contact with the child for a number of years.

If you don't want to serve the other parent, you may request that the notice requirement be waived. However, it's up to a judge to decide whether it's in the best interests of the child for the other parent to receive notice of the proposed name change. The judge might require that you search for the other parent before permitting a waiver of service, and the judge could even deny your request altogether. (The process for locating missing parents is covered in Section J of this chapter.)

To request that notice be waived, check the first box in this item. Check Item 10a to request that service be waived for the Applicant's father or Item 10b to request that service be waived for the Applicant's mother. Fill in the name of the father or mother in the appropriate blank. Then prepare an Attachment 10 following the guidelines in the accompanying sample.

**Item 11:** Check this box. If no additional pages are attached, fill in the word "None." If you are attaching any additional pages, count them and fill in the number of pages attached.

**Date and Signature:** In the spaces provided, fill in the date and print or type your present name. If there is a second Petitioner, print or type his name in the appropriate space. Sign the form on the designated signature line. Signing the document "under penalty of perjury" has the same effect as a sworn statement or oath, meaning you could be prosecuted under California law if you lie.

**Reminder:** If you are petitioning for name changes for more than one person, make sure you have completed a separate Attachment 2 for each one. All attachments should be stapled to the petition.

---

1  In the matter of the application of:

2  _____
   *[Name of Applicant(s)]*

3

4  <u>Attachment 10 to Petition for Change of Name</u>

5

6  *(Modify all that apply:)*

7  Applicant's father is unknown. He is not listed on Applicant's birth

8  certificate, a copy of which is attached to this document and incorporated

9  herein.

10  *(Or)*

11  Applicant's father and I were divorced on ____*[specify date]*____ and I do

12  not know his whereabouts. He was denied visitation rights of Applicant on

13  the basis of prior abuse and neglect and he has had no contact with her

14  since that date. A copy of the divorce decree is attached to this document

15  and incorporated herein.

16  *(Or)*

17  Applicant's father has had no contact with her since ____*[specify date]*____,

18  and has not made child support payments since ____*[specify date]*____. I have

19  remarried, and Applicant is known by the last name of her stepfather,

20  ____*[specify name]*____, who has acted as a father to her since ____*[specify date]*____.

21

22

## E. ORDER TO SHOW CAUSE FOR CHANGE OF NAME

THIS DOCUMENT WILL BE signed by a judge, then the information in it must be printed in a newspaper once a week for four weeks before the judge will decide whether to grant your name change. Once you've selected a newspaper for publication following the instructions in Section C, you're ready to complete the Order to Show Cause for Change of Name.

**Caption:** Follow the instructions in Section B3 of this chapter. If you checked Item 10 of the petition, check the box before the words "AND ORDER DISPENSING NOTICE."

**Item 1:** In the first blank, fill in your name, as well as anyone who is petitioning with you.

In the second set of blanks, fill in the Applicant's present name. After the word "to," fill in the Applicant's proposed name. If you are seeking name changes for more than one Applicant, fill in each of the present and proposed names. Always put the present name first, then the word "to" followed by the proposed name.

**Item 2a:** Do not fill in the information requested in the box. The clerk will complete this item when you file your documents with the court.

Underneath the box, after the words "located at (address of court)," fill in the court's complete street address, city and state.

**Item 2b:** Follow the instructions in Section C above for selecting a newspaper. Then fill in the full, complete name of the newspaper in the first blank. In the second blank, fill in the county where the newspaper is published—which must be the same county in which you are filing your petition.

**Item 2c:** If you checked Item 10 of the petition, complete this item in the same way.

**Date and Judge's Signature:** Leave these blank.

| PARTY WITHOUT AN ATTORNEY (*Name and Address*):<br>MOLLY MILLER and CLYDE MILLER  (916)555-1212<br>2863 East Ninth West Street<br>Sacramento, CA 95814<br><br>*In Pro Per* | TELEPHONE NO.: | *FOR COURT USE ONLY* |
|---|---|---|

**SUPERIOR COURT OF CALIFORNIA, COUNTY OF:**  SACRAMENTO
STREET ADDRESS: 720 Ninth Street, Room 103
MAILING ADDRESS:
CITY AND ZIP CODE: Sacramento, CA 95814
BRANCH NAME:

IN THE MATTER OF THE APPLICATION OF:

    JACK BLACK, a minor

| ORDER TO SHOW CAUSE FOR CHANGE OF NAME<br>☒ AND ORDER DISPENSING NOTICE | CASE NUMBER: |
|---|---|

1.   THE COURT FINDS that Petitioner(s) <u>MOLLY MILLER and CLYDE MILLER</u>

    has/have filed a Petition for Change of Name with the clerk of this court for an order changing Applicant(s)' name from

    <u>JACK BLACK</u>

    to  <u>JACK BLACK MILLER</u>

2.   THE COURT ORDERS:

    a. All people interested in this matter appear before this court to show cause why this application for change of name
       should not be granted on:

| Hearing date: | Time: | ☐ Dept.: | ☐ Div.: | ☐ Room: |
|---|---|---|---|---|

    located at (*address of court*):  720 Ninth Street, Sacramento, CA 95814

    b. A copy of this order to show cause be published once a week for four successive weeks prior to the day of said
       hearing in   <u>The Daily Recorder</u>  , a newspaper of
       general circulation printed in the County of <u>Sacramento</u>.

    c. ☒ Notice be dispensed with to the following person(s):

        1. ☒ Applicant's father (*name*): <u>MICHAEL BLACK</u>

        2. ☐ Applicant's mother (*name*): _____

Dated: ......................................    _____
                                         (Judge of the Superior Court)

*NP*         **ORDER TO SHOW CAUSE FOR CHANGE OF NAME**

## F. DECREE CHANGING NAME

ONCE A JUDGE APPROVES a name change, she signs a Decree Changing Name. The document is used to show that a legal name change has been granted.

If you are seeking a name change for more than one Applicant, prepare a separate Decree Changing Name for each person. Give information about each Applicant in a separate form.

**Caption:** Follow the instructions in Section B3 of this chapter.

**Item 1:** Fill in the Applicant's present name in the first set of blanks. After the word "to," fill in the Applicant's proposed new name.

**Items 1a-b:** Leave these items blank.

**Items 2a-c:** Leave these items blank.

**Item 3:** Fill in the Applicant's present name in the first set of blanks. After the word "to," fill in the Applicant's proposed new name.

**Date and Judge's Signature:** Leave these blank.

| PARTY WITHOUT AN ATTORNEY *(Name and Address)*: | TELEPHONE NO.: | FOR COURT USE ONLY |
|---|---|---|
| GERTRUDE WONG<br>24 Amador Way East<br>Hayward, CA 94544<br><br>*In Pro Per* | (415)555-1212 | |

**SUPERIOR COURT OF CALIFORNIA, COUNTY OF:** ALAMEDA
STREET ADDRESS: 24405 Amador Street
MAILING ADDRESS:
CITY AND ZIP CODE: Hayward, CA 94544
BRANCH NAME: Southern Division

IN THE MATTER OF THE APPLICATION OF:

GERTRUDE WONG

| **DECREE CHANGING NAME** | CASE NUMBER: |
|---|---|

1. The Petition for Change of Name for an order changing Applicant's name from _____

   GERTRUDE WONG
   _____

   to ____ GINA BEVERLY WONG _____

   came on for hearing as follows:

   a. Judge *(name)*:

   b. Hearing date:          Time:          ☐ Dept.:          ☐ Div.:          ☐ Room:

2. THE COURT FINDS:

   a. ☐ All notices required by law have been given.

   b. ☐ No objections were filed by any person.

   c. ☐ The allegations of the petition are sufficient and true.

3. THE COURT ORDERS:

   This petition be granted and that the name of Applicant be and is changed from _____

   __ GERTRUDE WONG _____

   to __ GINA BEVERLY WONG _____.

Dated: ..........................................................          _____

                                                              (Judge of the Superior Court)

*NP*                     **DECREE CHANGING NAME**

## G. ADDITIONAL DOCUMENTS MAY BE REQUIRED

YOU MAY NEED TO COMPLETE additional documents if:

- You are filing in a large county that has branch courts; or
- You have a very low income and are seeking a waiver of court fees.

    If neither of these applies, skip this section and go on to Section H.

### 1.  Certificate of Assignment

 In larger courts you must file a form that requests the court matter be assigned to a particular court branch. (In Section B1 above, you called the clerk to find out whether you should file in a branch court). The document is generally called a Certificate of Assignment or Declaration for Filing and Assignment. If you are filing in a branch court, call the court and arrange to get a copy of the local form. There are different local forms for different courts, but each form is self-explanatory. Refer to the accompanying sample as a guide.

    **Note**: Some courts may also require an initial filling form that gives brief information about the case. Check with the court.

# SUPERIOR COURT OF CALIFORNIA, COUNTY OF LOS ANGELES

In the matter of the application of:

HORACE SMITH

CASE NUMBER

## CERTIFICATE OF ASSIGNMENT

**File this certificate with all tort cases and all other civil actions or proceedings presented for filing in districts other than Central.**

[X] The undersigned declares that the above entitled matter is filed for proceedings in the EAST District of the Los Angeles Superior Court under Section 392 et seq., Code of Civil Procedure and Rule 300 Sections 3 and 4 of this court for the reasons checked below.

The address of the accident, performance, party, detention, place of business, or other factor which qualifies this case for filing in the above designated district is:

HORACE SMITH (Petitioner in pro per)          100 Mystreet
(NAME — INDICATE TITLE OR OTHER QUALIFYING FACTOR)          (ADDRESS)

Pomona                         CA                         91766
(CITY)                         (STATE)                         (ZIP CODE)

| | | NATURE OF ACTION | GROUND |
|---|---|---|---|
| ☐ | 1 | Abandonment | Petitioner resides within the district |
| ☐ | 2 | Adoption | Petitioner resides within the district |
| ☐ | 3 | Adoption | Consent to out-of-state adoption, consentor resides within the district |
| ☐ | 4 | Appeal from Labor Commission Decision | Labor hearing was held within the district |
| ☐ | 5 | Conservator | Petitioner or conservatee resides within the district |
| ☐ | 6 | Contract | Performance in the district is expressly provided for |
| ☐ | 7 | Equity | The cause of action arose within the district |
| ☐ | 8 | Eminent Domain | The property is located within the district |
| ☐ | 9 | Family Law | One or more of the party litigants resides within the district |
| ☐ | 10 | Forcible Entry | The property is located within the district |
| ☐ | 11 | Guardianship | Petitioner or ward resides within the district |
| ☐ | 12 | Habeas Corpus | No action pending, the person is held within the district |
| ☐ | 13 | Mandate* | The defendant functions wholly within the district |
| ☒ | 14 | Name Change | The petitioner resides within the district |
| ☐ | 15 | Personal Property | The property is located within the district |
| ☐ | 16 | Probate | Decedent resided or petitioner resides within the district |
| ☐ | 17 | Prohibition* | The defendant functions wholly within the district |
| ☐ | 18 | Review* | The defendant functions wholly within the district |
| ☐ | 19 | Small Claims Appeal | The lower court is located within the district |
| ☐ | 20 | Title to Real Property | The property is located within the district |
| ☐ | 21 | Tort | The cause of action arose within the district |
| ☐ | 22 | Tort | One or more defendant(s) reside within the district |
| ☐ | 23 | Transferred Action | The lower court is located within the district |
| ☐ | 24 | Unlawful Detainer | The property is located within the district |
| ☐ | 25 | _____ | Rule 300 allows filing in Central (non-torts only). |

I declare under penalty of perjury under the laws of the State of California that the foregoing is true and correct and this declaration was executed on May 2, 19__ at Pomona , California.

THE COURT MAY IMPOSE SANCTIONS OR OTHER PENALTIES FOR FAILURE TO FILE IN THE PROPER DISTRICT

*Horace Smith*
(SIGNATURE OF ATTORNEY)
HORACE SMITH, In Pro Per

* Prerogative writs concerning a court of inferior jurisdiction shall be filed in Central District.

**4**   76C134
RC 013/R8-89          CERTIFICATE OF ASSIGNMENT          RULE 300 LASCR

## 2.  Fee Waiver Documents

When you first file your documents, you will be required to pay a filing fee of $182. If you can afford to pay this fee, skip the rest of this section.

If you have a very low income, the court may order that you do not have to pay court fees and costs. You don't have to be absolutely destitute, but you really must be unable to pay. If you qualify to have court fees and costs waived and your financial situation later changes, you must immediately notify the court if you become able to pay. By law, you could be required to appear in court up to three years after you file for a fee waiver to answer questions about your ability to pay.

If you are currently receiving public assistance such as AFDC, Food Stamps, County Relief, General Relief, General Assistance, SSI or SSP, you should have no problem qualifying for the fee waiver. You should also qualify for a fee waiver if your gross monthly income (your monthly income before taxes or deductions are taken out) is equal to or less than the amounts shown in the accompanying chart.[6]

If your monthly income is higher than indicated in the chart but you can't afford to pay court fees, you must provide information about your monthly expenses. A judge will then review your financial situation and decide whether all or part of the expenses will be waived.

| Qualifying Income for Waiver of Court Fees and Costs | |
| --- | --- |
| **Number in Family** | **Monthly Family Income** |
| 1 | $ 709.38 |
| 2 | 957.30 |
| 3 | 1,205.21 |
| 4 | 1,453.13 |
| 5 | 1,701.05 |
| 6 | 1,948.96 |
| 7 | 2,196.88 |
| 8 | 2,444.80 |
| Each additional | 247.92 |

It's easy to apply for a waiver of court fees and costs. You simply complete two forms following the instructions in this section and file them along with the rest of your papers.

**Note:** Unfortunately, you cannot get a waiver of fees for the publication of your papers in a local newspaper.

### a.  Application for Waiver of Court Fees and Costs

 In this form, you explain why you cannot pay court fees, and request that they be waived.

---

[6]These figures were taken from the Judicial Council form "Information Sheet on Waiver of Court Fees and Costs," revised March 31, 1992 and were current as of 12/93. Check with the clerk to make sure the form—and the amounts listed—are up-to-date.

# — *THIS FORM MUST BE KEPT CONFIDENTIAL* —

| ATTORNEY OR PARTY WITHOUT ATTORNEY *(Name and Address)*: | TELEPHONE NO.: | FOR COURT USE ONLY |
|---|---|---|
| SYLVIA ANABELLE BARRETT<br>551 Main West Avenue<br>San Rafael, CA 94913 | (415)555-1212 | |

ATTORNEY FOR *(Name)* In Pro Per

NAME OF COURT Superior Court of Marin
STREET ADDRESS Hall of Justice, Room 151
MAILING ADDRESS P.O. Box E
CITY AND ZIP CODE San Rafael, CA 94913
BRANCH NAME

In the matter of the application of:

SYLVIA ANABELLE BARRETT

| APPLICATION FOR<br>WAIVER OF COURT FEES AND COSTS | CASE NUMBER: |
|---|---|

I request a court order so that I do not have to pay court fees and costs.

1. My address and date of birth are *(specify)*:

   551 Main West Avenue
   San Rafael, CA 94913

   4/2/41

2. [ ] I am receiving financial assistance under one or more of the following programs:
   a. [ ] **SSI and SSP:** The Supplemental Security Income and State Supplemental Payments Programs
   b. [ ] **AFDC:** The Aid to Families with Dependent Children Program
   c. [ ] **Food Stamps:** The Food Stamps Program
   d. [ ] **County Relief, General Relief (G.R.) or General Assistance (G.A.)**

*[If you checked box 2 above, sign at the bottom of this side and DO NOT fill out the rest of the form.]*

3. [X] My gross monthly income is less than the amount shown on the Information Sheet on Waiver of Court Fees and Costs available from the clerk's office.

*[If you checked box 3 above, skip 4, complete 5 and 6 on the back of this form, and sign at the bottom of this side.]*

4. [ ] My income is not enough to pay for the common necessaries of life for me and the people in my family I support and also pay court fees and costs. *[If you checked this box you must complete the back of this form.]*

---

**WARNING: You must immediately tell the court if you become able to pay court fees or costs during this action. For the next three (3) years you may be ordered to appear in court and answer questions about your ability to pay court fees or costs.**

---

I declare under penalty of perjury under the laws of the State of California that the foregoing is true and correct.

Date: September 16, 19___

SYLVIA ANABELLE BARRETT
*(TYPE OR PRINT NAME)*

*(SIGNATURE)*

---

**APPLICATION FOR WAIVER OF COURT FEES AND COSTS**
(In Forma Pauperis)
Gov. Code,
§ 68511.3

In the matter of the application of:

SYLVIA ANABELLE BARRETT

CASE NUMBER:

## FINANCIAL INFORMATION

5. [X] My pay changes considerably from month to month. *(If you check this box, each of the amounts reported in 6 should be your average for the past 12 months.)*

6. My monthly income:

a. My gross monthly pay is: . . . . . . . . $ 600.00

b. My payroll deductions are *(specify purpose and amount)*:

(1) _____ $ _____

(2) _____ $ _____

(3) _____ $ _____

(4) _____ $ _____

My TOTAL payroll deduction amount is: $ _-0-_

c. My monthly take-home pay is *(a. minus b.)*: . . . . . . . . . . . . . . . $ 600.00

d. Other money I get each month is *(specify source and amount)*:

(1) _____ $ _____

(2) _____ $ _____

The TOTAL amount of other money is: $ _-0-_

e. **MY TOTAL MONTHLY INCOME IS** *(c. plus d.)*: . . . . . . . . . . . . . . . . . $ 600.00

f. **The number of people in my family, including me, supported by this money is:** __1__

7.  a. [ ] I am *not* able to pay any of the court fees and costs.

b. [ ] I am able to pay *only* the following court fees and costs *(specify)*:

8. My monthly expenses are:

a. Rent or house payment & maintenance $ _____

b. Food and household supplies . . . . . . $ _____

c. Utilities and telephone . . . . . . . . . . $ _____

d. Clothing . . . . . . . . . . . . . . . . . . . $ _____

e. Laundry and cleaning . . . . . . . . . . . $ _____

f. Medical and dental payments . . . . . . $ _____

g. Insurance (life, health, accident, etc.) $ _____

h. School, child care . . . . . . . . . . . . . $ _____

i. Child, spousal support (prior marriage) $ _____

j. Transportation and auto expenses (insurance, gas, repair) . . . . . . . . . $ _____

k. Installment payments *(specify purpose and amount)*:

(1) _____ $ _____

(2) _____ $ _____

(3) _____ $ _____

The TOTAL amount of monthly installment payments is: . . . . . . . . $ _____

l. Amounts deducted due to wage assignments and earnings withholding orders $ _____

m. Other expenses *(specify)*

(1) _____ $ _____

(2) _____ $ _____

(3) _____ $ _____

(4) _____ $ _____

(5) _____ $ _____

(6) _____ $ _____

The TOTAL amount of other monthly expenses is: . . . . . . . . . . . . . . . $ _____

n. **MY TOTAL MONTHLY EXPENSES ARE** *(add a. through m.)*: . . . . . . . . . . . $ _____

9. I own the following property:

a. Cash . . . . . . . . . . . . . . . . . . . . . $ _____

b. Checking, savings and credit union accounts *(list banks)*:

(1) _____ $ _____

(2) _____ $ _____

(3) _____ $ _____

c. Cars, other vehicles and boat equity *(list make, year of each)*:

(1) _____ $ _____

(2) _____ $ _____

(3) _____ $ _____

d. Real estate equity . . . . . . . . . . . . . $ _____

e. Other personal property -- jewelry, furniture, furs, stocks, bonds, etc. *(list separately)*:

$ _____

10. Other facts which support this application are *(describe unusual medical needs, expenses for recent family emergencies, or other unusual expenses to help the judge understand your budget)*. If more space is needed, attach page labeled attachment 10.

WARNING: You must immediately tell the court if you become able to pay court fees or costs during this action. For the next three (3) years you may be ordered to appear in court and answer questions about your ability to pay court fees or costs.

982(a)(17) (Rev. January 1, 1985)

**APPLICATION FOR WAIVER OF COURT FEES AND COSTS**
(In Forma Pauperis)

Page two

**Caption:** Follow the instructions in Section B3 of this chapter.

**Item 1:** Fill in your present address and the date you were born.

**Item 2:** If you are receiving public assistance of any kind, check the first box.

**Items 2a-d:** Check all the boxes that tell which kind of public assistance you are receiving.

**Important**: If you checked Item 2, do not complete the rest of the form. Simply fill in the date at the bottom of the front page, print or type your present name in the space provided at the left and sign the form on the signature line.

**Item 3:** Check this box if your gross monthly income (the amount you receive before any taxes or deductions are taken out) is less than the amount shown in the chart entitled "Qualifying Income for Waiver of Court Fees and Costs" above.

**Important**: If you checked Item 3, skip Item 4, and complete only Items 5 and 6 on the back of the form. Sign and date the form on this page.

**Item 4:** Skip this item if you checked Item 2 or Item 3. Otherwise, check this box if you believe that you are genuinely unable—rather than unwilling—to pay court fees and costs. If you check Item 4, you must complete the entire back side of the form.

**Caption for Page Two:** Fill in the name of the Applicant(s). Leave the case number blank since it hasn't been assigned yet.

**Item 5:** Check this box if the amount of your earnings changes a great deal each month, such as if you are self-employed and make a fair amount of money one month but little another month. If you check this item, use averages for each of the figures required in Item 6. For example, to get a monthly average of your income for the last year, add up your total earnings for the last 12 months and divide that amount by 12.

**Item 6a:** Fill in the amount of your gross monthly pay. This is the income you receive each month before any taxes or deductions are taken out.

**Items 6b(1)-(4):** Fill in the type and amount of each of your payroll deductions in the spaces provided. Then add together all of the amounts you listed in Items 6b(1)-(4) and fill in the total payroll deduction amount.

**Item 6c:** Subtract the total payroll deductions from your gross monthly pay: Item 6a minus the total of Items 6b(1)-(4). Fill in this amount.

**Item 6d:** Fill in information about other money you get each month, such as spousal support, in Items 6d(1)-(2). Then fill in the total amount of additional money you receive each month after adding together the amounts you listed in Items 6d(1)-(2).

**Item 6e:** Add together Items 6c and 6d and enter this amount.

**Item 6f:** Fill in the total number of people in your family you are supporting with the amount of money you have listed in Item 6e. Remember to count yourself as one of them.

**Items 7-10:** Skip all of these items (Items 7-10) unless you checked Item 4 on the front of this form.

**Item 7:** Only check one of the two boxes listed in this item.

**Item 7a:** Check this box if you believe that you can't pay any of the court filing fees and costs.

**Item 7b:** Check this box if you believe that you can only pay part of the court filing fees and costs. Then fill in the amount you believe you can pay.

**Items 8a-m:** In these items you tell how much you pay each month in living expenses. Make sure you list all of your expenses.

**Item 8n:** Add together all of the amounts you filled in for Items 8a-8m for your monthly expenses and enter this amount.

**Items 9a-e:** Fill in the estimated value of any property you own, including money, vehicles, real estate and personal property.

**Item 10:** Fill in this item if there is any reason why you can't pay court fees and costs. This might include unusual medical expenses, money spent for recent family emergencies or other unusual expenses. You will need to attach an additional page to the Application for Waiver of Court Fees and Costs to provide this information. In your own words, explain why you cannot pay the court fees and costs.

**Important:** If you have not already dated and signed the form on the first page, do this now.

### b. Order on Application for Waiver of Court Fees and Costs

 A judge must sign this form to give permission for your court fees and costs to be waived.

**Caption:** Follow the instructions in Section B3 of this chapter.

After you fill in the caption, just list your name, the same as on the caption in Item 1b. Leave the rest of the front side of the form blank; the court clerk and judge will complete it. Then turn to the back of the form.

**Caption for Page Two:** Fill in the name of the Applicant(s). Leave the case number blank since it hasn't been assigned yet.

At the bottom of the page, after the clerk's certification, fill in your full name and complete mailing address. You have now completed your part of the form. The rest will be completed by the court clerk.

| ATTORNEY OR PARTY WITHOUT ATTORNEY (Name and Address) | TELEPHONE NO | FOR COURT USE ONLY |
|---|---|---|
| BENJAMIN JONATHAN LEE<br>9403 Main Street<br>Oakland, CA 94612 | (415)555-1212 | |
| ATTORNEY FOR (Name) In Pro Per | | |

NAME OF COURT, JUDICIAL DISTRICT OR BRANCH COURT, IF ANY

SUPERIOR COURT OF ALAMEDA, NORTHERN DIVISION

In the matter of the application of:
BENJAMIN JONATHAN LEE

| ORDER ON APPLICATION FOR WAIVER<br>OF COURT FEES AND COSTS | CASE NUMBER: |
|---|---|

1. The application was filed
   a. on (date):
   b. by (name): Benjamin Jonathan Lee
2. ☐ IT IS ORDERED THAT the application is granted and the applicant is permitted to proceed in this action **as follows:**
   a. ☐ without payment of any court fees or costs listed in rule 985(i), California Rules of Court.
   b. ☐ without payment of any court fees or costs listed in rule 985(i), California Rules of Court, except the following:

   c. ☐ without payment of the following court fees or costs (specify):

   d. The reasons for denial of any requested waiver are (specify):

   e. ☐ The clerk of the court is directed to mail a copy of this order to the applicant's attorney, if any, or to the applicant if unrepresented.
   f. ☐ All unpaid fees and costs shall be deemed to be taxable costs if applicant is entitled to costs and shall be a lien on any judgment recovered by the applicant and shall be paid to the clerk upon such recovery.
3. ☐ IT IS ORDERED THAT the application is denied for the following reasons (specify):

   a. **The applicant must pay any fees and costs due in this action within ten days from the date of service of this order or any paper filed by the applicant with the clerk will be of no effect.**
   b. The clerk of the court is directed to mail a copy of this order to all parties who have appeared in this action.
4. ☐ IT IS ORDERED THAT a hearing be held.
   a. The substantial evidentiary conflict to be resolved by the hearing is (specify):

   b. Applicant should be present at the hearing to be held:

| hearing date: | time: | in ☐ Dept.: | ☐ Div.: | ☐ Rm.: |
|---|---|---|---|---|
| address of court: | | | | |

   c. The clerk of the court is directed to mail a copy of this order to the applicant only.

Dated: . . . . . . . . . . . . . . . . . . . . . . . . _____
(Clerk's certification on page 2)     (Signature of Judge)

| Form Adopted by Rule 982<br>Judicial Council of California<br>Revised effective July 1, 1981 | ORDER ON APPLICATION FOR WAIVER<br>OF COURT FEES AND COSTS<br>(IN FORMA PAUPERIS) | Govt Code<br>§ 68511 3 |

In the matter of the application of:
BENJAMIN JONATHAN LEE

CASE NUMBER:

**ORDER ON APPLICATION FOR WAIVER OF COURT FEES AND COSTS**     Page 2

**CLERK'S CERTIFICATE OF MAILING**

I certify that I am not a party to this cause and that a copy of the foregoing was mailed first class, postage prepaid, in a sealed envelope addressed as shown below, and that the mailing of the foregoing and execution of this certificate occurred at (place):. . . . . . . . . . . . . . . . . . . . . . . . . . . . . . . . . . . . . . . . . . , California,

on (date): . . . . . . . . . . . . . . . . . . . . Clerk, by _____
(Deputy) .

**CLERK'S CERTIFICATION**

(SEAL)

I certify that the foregoing is a true copy of the original on file in my office.

Dated:. . . . . . . . . . . . . Clerk, by . . . . . . . . . . . . . . .
(Deputy)

Benjamin Jonathan Lee
9403 Main Street
Oakland, CA 94612

## H. COPY AND FILE PAPERS WITH COURT

MAKE AT LEAST THREE PHOTOCOPIES of all the documents you've prepared. If a form is two or more pages long, staple the pages together. If you are seeking a name change for your child and the child's other parent has not signed the petition, you'll need one more photocopy of the documents for the other parent. Some courts also require an extra copy or two—you can call the Superior Court clerk and find out.[7] (See Section B1 of this chapter for information on calling the court clerk.)

---

### Rules, Glorious Rules!

Some courts are particular about the way documents are prepared and filed, and might refuse to accept papers that don't exactly comply with those requirements. You can check with the Superior Court clerk about these rules:

- How many copies of each document are required. Most courts require only the original, but some require an additional one or two copies.

- Whether documents must be two-hole punched. Some courts prefer this, and others require it.

- Whether documents may be folded. Although it may seem ridiculous, a few courts have policies not to accept folded documents.

- Whether original documents must be marked with the word "original" and copies must be marked with the word "copy." Some courts prefer this, and others require it.

- Whether "bluebacks" are required. This is blue paper which is stapled to the backs of documents. It identifies the people involved in the legal action, the court and the nature of the document being filed. Courts that require bluebacks, such as Los Angeles County, usually require them only on forms that are not preprinted—so you probably won't need them. Bluebacks can be obtained from most large office supply stores.

---

[7]If there is no newspaper in your county, you'll need three extra copies of the Order to Show Cause for Change of Name for filing with the court clerk.

### 1. Take or Mail Papers to Court

You file documents simply by taking or sending them to the Superior Court clerk. If you go to court in person, take along the original and copies of your documents as well as two self-addressed, stamped envelopes. Take a checkbook or fee waiver documents.

If you mail the documents, write a letter using the accompanying sample as a guide, and send it along with the filing fee or fee waiver documents and two self-addressed, stamped envelopes. Regardless of whether you take your papers in person or mail them, it's a good idea to leave an extra copy of everything at home in case the papers are lost or misplaced.

What happens when you file your papers with the court is really quite simple. When you deliver your papers to the court, you pay a filing fee or apply for a fee waiver following the instructions in Section H2 below. Your case is assigned a number and a new file is opened. The clerk files the petition in your case file, and may also keep one or two photocopies, depending on the county policy. You get back any extra copies with rubber-stamped information in the upper right-hand corner of the document showing the date that the original was filed.

The clerk also assigns a hearing date—usually about six weeks from the date you file your papers. In some larger counties, you may have to get a court date from a different person, called the "calendar clerk." The clerk completes information about the date, time and location of the hearing in the box provided for this purpose in the Order to Show Cause. Although you probably won't need to attend the hearing, make sure you can appear at the date and time the clerk assigns. If you won't be able to attend, ask the clerk for a different hearing date.

The clerk may keep the Order to Show Cause for approval and signature by a judge. Either leave a self-addressed, stamped envelope with the clerk or make arrangements to come back later and pick up a signed copy. The Decree Changing Name will not be stamped and returned to you. That's because a judge must first sign the document, which will happen on the hearing date several weeks away.

---

November 11, 19___

County Clerk
Superior Court of California
County of San Diego
P.O. Box 128
San Diego, CA 92112-4104

Dear Clerk:

I have enclosed:
1) Original and 4 copies of: Petition for Change of Name; Order to Show Cause; and Decree Changing Name.
2) Check in the amount of $___; and
4) Two self-addressed, stamped envelopes.

Please file these papers, provide me with a hearing date and return date-stamped copies to me in one of the enclosed self-addressed, stamped envelopes. The second envelope is included for mailing a copy of the decree to me after the hearing.

Sincerely,

*Bessie Johnson*
Bessie Johnson
1 Main Street
San Diego, CA 92101
Phone: (619) 555-1212

---

## 2.  Applying for Waiver of Court Fees and Costs

Skip this section unless you have a very low income and are applying to have court fees and costs waived. If so, make sure you have prepared and copied the documents set out in Section G2 of this chapter.

By law, you may file your petition with the court at the same time as the fee waiver request, without paying a filing fee. Some clerks may tell you that you'll have to wait a few days for a judge to grant the fee waiver before you can file your papers. If this happens, be polite but firm. Tell the clerk that you are entitled to file your petition under Rule 985(a) of the California Rules of Court. If for some reason the clerk still will not file your papers, ask to speak with a supervisor.

If you file your documents in person, you may have to take the fee waiver documents to be reviewed and filed by a clerk in a different department or courtroom from the regular filing desk. To find out the procedure for filing fee waiver documents, check with the court clerk.

Once an Application for Waiver of Court Fees and Costs form has been filed, the court must decide whether to grant the request within five days. If the court doesn't deny your request within that five-day period, your fees and costs are automatically waived (California Rules of Court Rule 985(e)). The court might send you a document entitled "Notice of Waiver of Court Fees and Costs," which indicates that your request was granted. However, in the real world, courts usually don't send out this form. If you don't get any notification from the court within a week after you file your documents, call the clerk to find out whether your fees were waived.

If your fee waiver request is denied, the Order on Waiver of Court Fees and Costs will be marked to indicate this. You will then have to pay the filing fee within 10 days.

## I.  ARRANGE PUBLICATION

AFTER YOU FILE YOUR PAPERS with the court, take a copy of the officially stamped Order to Show Cause to the newspaper you selected. The newspaper will publish the Order to Show Cause once a week for four weeks. It will then send a form—called an Affidavit of Publication—to the court verifying that the order was published as required. Ask the newspaper to send the affidavit directly to the court, with a copy to you. Double check that the affidavit was sent to the court by calling the newspaper a few days after the last publishing date.

**Note:** If there is no newspaper published in your county, the clerk of the court may post the order in three of the most public places in the county (Code of Civil Procedure §1277). You'll need to give three file-stamped copies of the Order to Show Cause to the clerk and request the posting. Ask the court clerk to file a proof of posting in your case when the posting is complete.

## J.  SERVICE MAY BE REQUIRED FOR MINOR'S NAME CHANGE

SKIP THIS ENTIRE SECTION and go on to Section K unless the name change is for a minor. Both living parents are entitled to know about the proposed name change of their child Sometimes a judge will waive the notice requirement, if requested in the petition. (See the instructions for Item 10 of the petition set out in Section D of this chapter.)

If only one living parent signs the petition and does not request a waiver of the notice requirement, the other parent must be formally notified at least 30 days before the scheduled hearing (Code of Civil Procedure §1277(a)). The notification must be done through a special procedure called "service of process."

**Note:** Even if you requested a wavier of the notice requirement, a judge must decide whether it's in the best interests of the child. See the instructions for Item 10 of the petition contained in Section D of this chapter.

If possible, enlist the other parent's support in the name change. Like it or not, the other parent has a legal right to contest the name change. You'll probably find it easier to be polite with the other parent instead of antagonizing him into fighting the name change in court. Of course, you'll need to use your own judgment. For example, if the other parent will evade service if he knows about it in advance, but won't contest the name change, you might not want to let him know about your plans.

### Laws Governing Service on Minor's Parent

It used to be that the court clerk was responsible for mailing notice of the name change to a minor's parent if only one parent signed the name change petition. Typically the petitioning parent supplied the clerk with an extra copy of the Order to Show Cause and a stamped envelope addressed to the other parent.

Code of Civil Procedure §1277(a) now requires that service be done personally if the other parent lives in California. If the other parent lives outside of California, service may be done either personally or by certified mail, return receipt requested.

### 1.  What is "Service of Process?"

When someone personally delivers or sends legal documents by mail to a person named in a court proceeding, this formal notice is called "service of process." The person who receives the documents is "served." Service of process cannot be done by the person petitioning for the name change. Specific rules about how service must be done to be legally valid are explained in the rest of this section. If service is not done properly, the name change will not be granted on the hearing date.

### 2.  How to Have Other Parent Served

Unless the other parent signed the petition, he must be served personally with a copy of the Order to Show Cause unless he lives outside of California, where he may be served personally or by certified U.S. mail, return receipt requested. The other parent must be served at least 30 days before the scheduled hearing date. The Order to Show Cause must have the date, time and location of the hearing marked on it.

The law forbids you—the person petitioning for the name change—from serving the papers yourself. But service can be carried out by any other person 18 years of age or older who is not signing the name change petition. This might be a friend, family member, acquaintance or employee. Or, for a fee, you can hire a professional process server or marshal or sheriff's deputy to serve the papers. Once documents are served, you will need to complete a short form stating that service was completed, and the process server must sign it.

#### a.  Personal Service if Other Parent in California

If the other parent lives in California, a copy of the Order to Show Cause must be handed to or left for him by a process server. The other parent may be served at home, work or any other place. However, it's usually recommended that the other parent be served at home, so she is not interrupted at her job. If you have service of process done by an adult relative, neighbor or friend, give careful instructions about the legal requirements for serving papers.

The server must personally give copies of the Order to Show Cause to the other parent at least 30 days before the scheduled hearing date. Even if the other parent won't accept the papers, service can still be completed. Once the process server sees the other parent, makes personal identification, and is close enough to make the service, it doesn't matter if the other parent refuses to take the papers, gets angry, or tries to run away. The server can put the papers on the ground as close as possible to the other parent's feet, saying something like "This is for you," or "You have been served," and leave.

Under no circumstance should the process server pick up the papers once they have been served in this manner. If he does, the service will be invalidated and have to be done again. He should never try to force the other parent to take the papers—it's unnecessary and may subject the process server (or even you) to a lawsuit for battery. Your server should understand that personal service is not complete if he simply leaves the papers with anyone except the other parent, on the porch or in the mailbox (which, incidentally, is illegal under Postal Service regulations).

If you use a process serving firm in the area where the other parent lives, you may want to get a recommendation from a paralegal or attorney, if you know one. You can look in the Yellow Pages for process servers and call around to check fees. You will need to give the process server copies of the Order to Show Cause and the date by which service must be completed, which is 30 days before the scheduled hearing date. Since the process server won't be familiar with the person she's serving, you'll need to help out by providing as much detailed information as possible, such as the best hours to find the other parent at home and a detailed physical description. It's even better if you can provide the process server with a recent photograph of the other parent.

If you want to have a marshal or deputy serve the papers, call the marshal's office or civil division of the county sheriff's office to find out who serves court papers in your county. Then send or take to that office copies of the Order to Show Cause, pay a fee (usually about $20), and fill out a form giving a physical description of the other parent and other information, such as the best hours to find the other parent at home or work.

### b. Service if Other Parent Out-of-State

If the other parent lives outside of California, service can be accomplished in either of these ways:

- At least 30 days before the scheduled hearing date, the other parent must be personally served; or

- At least 40 days before the hearing, the other parent must be sent notice by certified mail, return receipt requested. If service is by certified mail, it is probably valid only if the other parent signs and sends the receipt back to you.

To have the parent served by mail, place a copy of the file-stamped Order to Show Cause in an envelope and put the other parent's name and address on it. Then go to your local post office—or have your process server go with you—and fill in the forms necessary to send these documents by certified mail and pay the required postage.

You cannot send the papers yourself. However, a friend or relative over age 18 can simply drop the envelope in a mailbox. It's fine to use a non-professional if service is made through the mail.

If the other parent accepts the documents, you will receive your return receipt back in the mail. Keep the signed return receipt in a safe place. You will need to file it along with a proof of service, following the instructions in Section J2c below.

Should the other parent refuse to accept the certified envelope, you may need to:

- arrange for personal service (see Section J2a above); or

- request that service be waived (see Section J3 of this chapter).

**Note:** If the other person is in the military, you may petition for the change, but the other parent can contest it at a later time if he didn't get a chance to object at the time of the hearing.

### c. Complete and File Proof of Service

Once the other parent has been served, complete a Proof of Service. This form is a declaration by someone (other than you) stating how and when documents were served. After the form is filled in, the person who served the papers must sign it.

**Caption:** Follow the instructions in Section B3 of this chapter. Carefully copy the case number from papers you've already filed.

**Item 1:** Leave this item blank. It simply states that the person who served the documents is at least 18 years old and not involved in the name change case.

**Item 2:** Fill in the business or residence address of the person who served the documents.

**Item 3a:** Check this box if the other parent was personally served. If the other parent was served by certified mail, skip this item and go on to Item 3b.

**Item 3a(1):** Fill in the name of the other parent.

**Item 3a(2):** Fill in the address where the other parent was served.

**Item 3a(3):** Fill in the date the other parent was served.

**Item 3a(4):** Fill in the approximate time the other parent was served.

**Item 3b:** Check this box if the other parent lives out-of-state and was served by certified mail, return receipt requested. Skip this item if the other parent was personally served, and go on to Item 4.

**Item 3b(1):** Fill in the name of the other parent.

**Item 3b(2):** Fill in the address to which the Order to Show Cause was mailed.

**Item 3b(3):** Fill in the date the Order to Show Cause was mailed.

**Item 3b(4):** Fill in the city and state where the Order to Show Cause was mailed.

**Item 3b(5):** Staple to the Proof of Service the original return receipt which the other parent signed when he received the documents. Keep a copy of the return receipt for your records.[8]

**Item 4:** Leave this item blank.

Have the person who served the documents fill in the date, print or type her full name on the line provided and sign the form on the signature line.

Finally, at least one week before the scheduled hearing date, file the Proof of Service with the court. Remember to keep copies for your files.

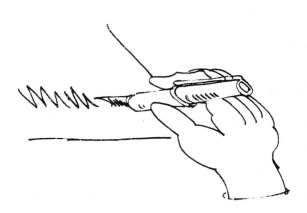

---

[8]If the other parent refuses to accept the mail or you don't receive the return receipt in the mail, the judge may require that you submit a declaration explaining the situation. Or the judge may insist that you attempt service again. (See Section J3 of this chapter.)

PARTY WITHOUT AN ATTORNEY (*Name and Address*):

MARIA RIVERA
20 20th Street
Los Angeles, CA 90053

*In Pro Per*

TELEPHONE NO.: (213)555-1212

FOR COURT USE ONLY

**SUPERIOR COURT OF CALIFORNIA, COUNTY OF:** LOS ANGELES
STREET ADDRESS: 111 North Hill Street
MAILING ADDRESS: P.O. Box 151
CITY AND ZIP CODE: Los Angeles, CA 90053
BRANCH NAME:

IN THE MATTER OF THE APPLICATION OF:

MANUEL LOPEZ, a minor

**PROOF OF SERVICE (NAME CHANGE)**

CASE NUMBER: 2222

I declare that:

1. At the time of service I was at least 18 years of age and not a party to this legal action.

2. My business or residence address is: 4 West Main Street, Los Angeles, California 90053

3. I served copies of the Order to Show Cause for Change of Name in the manner shown (*check either a or b below*):

   a. ☐ **Personal Service.** I personally delivered these papers to:

      (1) Name of person served: _____

      (2) Address where served: _____

      _____

      (3) Date served: _____

      (4) Time served: _____

   b. ☒ **Certified mail, return receipt requested.** I deposited these papers in the United States mail, in a sealed envelope with postage fully prepaid. I used certified mail and requested a return receipt. The envelope was addressed and mailed to:

      (1) Name of person served: Frank Lopez

      (2) Address to which documents were mailed: P.O. Box A-1
      Cleveland, Ohio 44118

      (3) Date documents were mailed: April 12, 19__

      (4) City and state where mailing occurred: Los Angeles, California

      (5) The signed return receipt is attached.

4. I declare under penalty of perjury under the laws of the State of California that the foregoing is true and correct.

Date: April 17, 19__

WANDA WASHINGTON
.................................................
(Type or Print Name of Process Server)

*Wanda Washington*
_____
Signature of Process Server

*NP*

**PROOF OF SERVICE (NAME CHANGE)**

### 3.  If You Cannot Find Other Parent

You'll obviously find it difficult to have the other parent served if you do not know his whereabouts and cannot locate him.

If you anticipated problems with service, you probably completed Item 10 of the Petition for Change of Name in Section D of this chapter. But perhaps you thought it would be easy to locate the other parent. Or maybe you thought you knew the other parent's current address, but it turned out to be incorrect.

You'll need to do your best to find and have the other parent served. A judge will then decide whether to waive the notice requirement or insist that you publish notice in a newspaper the other parent is most likely to see. Local rules for this procedure vary, so you'll need to check with your court to find out the custom.

Follow instructions for preparing appropriate documents set out below. Type your documents on lined pleading paper. (A blank sheet is provided in Appendix 2.) Make photocopies and file your documents with the court according to local rules—usually at least several days before the hearing date.

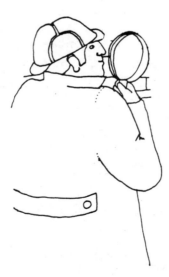

### a.  How to Search for Other Parent

You may search for the other parent by yourself or get help from others, such as adult friends or relatives. Keep a written record of the search and include the date each attempt was made. If you send any letters, keep copies of correspondence. Before waiving notice, courts often require that you contact these sources:

- *Telephone Company:* Check telephone directories and Directory Assistance in cities where the other parent has lived recently. Most public libraries carry copies of telephone directories for many large cities, including areas outside of California.

- *Friends, Relatives and Former Employers:* Contact the other parent's relatives and friends to see if they have leads on his whereabouts. If you know where the other parent used to work, contact former employers to find out if they have an address, telephone number, or the name of someone else who might know how to locate the other parent.

- *Last Known Address:* If the other parent has moved and left a forwarding address, you can obtain it from the U.S. Post Office. Send a post card or envelope to the last known address with the words "Address Correction Requested" printed next to the old address, and list your return address on the envelope. You might check with the people living at the other parent's last known address and the neighbors on both sides. If the last known address is a mental or penal institution, find out whether the institution's records are confidential or if you can obtain the other parent's current address.

- *Voter Registration Records:* In California, you can find listings for registered voters which includes their name, address and phone number. To look at these records, contact the registrar of voters for the county where you believe the relative lives. If the other parent has moved within the same county, the registrar may have the new address.

- *Department of Motor Vehicles:* If the other parent lives outside of California, contact the motor vehicle department in that state to find out how to obtain information on registered vehicles and drivers. If the other parent lives in California, the California Department of Motor Vehicles (DMV) will not release address information without first contacting the other parent—all of which takes a minimum of several weeks. For a fee, the DMV checks for an exact match of the name you provide. If you're willing to pay for separate name searches, you could submit several requests with variations of the other parent's name—for example, John P. Smith, J.P. Smith and John Paul Smith. Contact your local DMV office or write to the DMV, Division of Driver's Licenses, P.O. Box 2590, Sacramento, CA 95812.

- *Military Services:* If you think the other parent is a member of the military, write to the personnel records branch of the appropriate military branch in Washington, D.C. You'll need to pay a fee (approximately $15), and request information as to whether or not the other parent is on active duty in that branch of the military service.

**b. Due Diligence Declaration**

If you cannot find the other parent, you will need to let the court know what steps you took in your search. You state this in a Due Diligence Declaration. If anyone helped search, prepare a separate declaration for each person and have them sign the document. Follow the guidelines of the following sample:

[YOUR NAME in caps]
[your street address]
[your city, state and zip]
[your phone number, including area code]

Petitioner In Pro Per

SUPERIOR COURT OF CALIFORNIA

COUNTY OF [COUNTY in caps, followed by branch name, if any]

In the matter of the application of:  ) Case No. [Case No.]
                                      )
                                      ) DUE DILLIGENCE DECLARATION
[NAME OF APPLICANT(S) in caps:        )
indicate if applicant is a minor]     )

I, [your name or name of person who searched for missing parent], declare that I am [if you
"the Petitioner in this case" or state relationship, such as "the sister of Applicant and friend of Petitioner"]. I
have made the following attempts to locate [name of missing parent], who is
Applicant's ["mother" or "father"], but to date my efforts have been unsuccessful. The details of my

1. I checked in telephone directories for listings. The details of my
attempts are: [list the date each attempt was made, the city of the telephone directory and the results of the
search, such as no one was listed under that name, or you called and it was the wrong person].

2. I checked with directory assistance. The details of my attempts are:
[list the date each attempt was made, the city or area code that was called and the results of the search, such as no
one was listed under that name, or you called and it was the wrong person].

3. I checked with friends and relatives. The details of my attempts are:
[list the date each attempt was made, the name and relationship to the missing parent of each person contacted and
the results of the search, such as a friend didn't know the whereabouts of the missing parent, or a brother gave a
disconnected telephone number for the missing parent].

4. I checked with former employers. The details of my attempts are: [list

-1-

the date each attempt was made, the name of each former employer contacted and the results of the search, such as
the former employer had fired the missing parent and didn't know where he'd gone, or the former employer had the
forwarding address of a business which went bankrupt two years ago].

5. I checked the last known residence address. The details of my attempts
are: [list the date each attempt was made and the results of the search, such as you went to the house and the
missing parent was no longer living there and the tenant didn't know where he had moved, or the post office did not
have a forwarding address on file].

6. I checked with voter registration records. The details of my attempts
are: [list the date each attempt was made, the county and state of each registrar of voters contacted and the
results of the search, such as the missing parent was not registered to vote, or was no longer at the address listed].

7. I checked with the motor vehicles department. The details of my
attempts are: [list the date each attempt was made, the state in which the motor vehicles department was
contacted and the results of the search, such as the missing parent was not registered with the motor vehicles
department, or there was no current address listed].

8. [List information about any other search attempts, including the date each attempt was made and a
detailed description of the results of the search, such as you checked with the army and there was no forwarding
address on file, or you checked with the court where the missing parent had filed a lawsuit and there was no current
address listed in the court's files].

I declare under penalty of perjury under the laws of the State of
California that the foregoing is true and correct.

Dated: [today's date]     _____
                          [your name or name of person who searched for missing parent]

-2-

## c. Waiver of Notice

If you don't want to serve the other parent, you'll need to obtain a judge's permission. Depending on local rules, this may take place either before or on the hearing date—which would then be postponed. Prepare a Due Diligence Declaration following the instructions in Section J3b above. Then prepare an Application and Order Dispensing Notice re: Change of Name, using the accompanying sample as a guide.

```
1   [YOUR NAME in caps]
    [your street address]
2   [your city, state and zip]
    [your phone number, including area code]
3
    Petitioner In Pro Per
4

5

6

7

8               SUPERIOR COURT OF CALIFORNIA
9        COUNTY OF  [COUNTY in caps, followed by branch name, if any]
10

11  In the matter of the application of:  ) Case No. [Case No.]
                                          )
12  [NAME OF APPLICANT(S) in caps;        ) APPLICATION AND ORDER DISPENSING
    indicate if applicant is a minor]     ) WITH NOTICE RE: CHANGE OF NAME
13  _____)

14      Application is hereby made for an order dispensing with notice to [full

15  name of other parent], the ["mother" or "father"] of minor Applicant [minor's present name] in

16  this name change proceeding. The whereabouts of [full name of other parent] are

17  unknown to the Petitioner. Attempts to locate [full name of other parent] are set out

18  in detail in the Due Diligence Declaration(s) filed in support of this

19  application. Petitioner requests that the court issue an order dispensing with

20  notice to [full name of other parent] .

21  Dated: [today's date]

22                                  _____
                                    [your name]
23

24      IT IS THE ORDER OF THIS COURT that notice to [full name of parent] , the

25  ["mother" or "father"] of Applicant [minor's present name], be dispensed with.

26  Dated:

27                                  _____
                                    Judge of the Superior Court
28
```

### d. Service by Publication

If the other parent's whereabouts are unknown, you may need to publish a copy of the Order to Show Cause in the county where the other parent is most likely to get notice. Some courts have a local notice of hearing form that must be published instead. Depending on local rules, a judge may decide on the publication requirement either before or on the hearing date—which would then be postponed.

Prepare a Due Diligence Declaration following the instructions in Section J3b above. Then prepare an Application and Order for Publication using the accompanying sample as a guide.

**Note:** Since you've already published notice in the county where the minor lives, additional publication may not be required if the other parent probably lives in the same county. If so, modify the accompanying form to show that.

Make photocopies and file your papers with the court. After a judge has signed the Order for Publication, arrange to get copies from the court by either providing a self-addressed, stamped envelope or picking up the documents. At least four weeks before the scheduled hearing date, have a copy of the Order to Show Cause or notice of hearing published in the newspaper listed in the Order for Publication. Follow the basic instructions for having the notice published set out in Section I of this chapter.

You're generally required to have a copy of the Order to Show Cause or notice of hearing mailed to the other parent. If you don't have an address for the other parent, prepare a Declaration of Inability to Ascertain Address. Use the accompanying sample as a guide.

If you have an address for the other parent, have an adult mail a copy of the document specified in the signed order to the other parent as soon as possible before the scheduled hearing date. The document should be sent by regular U.S. mail. Do not mail the papers yourself. Then prepare a Proof of Service by Mail and have the person who mailed notice sign it. Use the accompanying sample as a guide.

1    *[YOUR NAME in caps]*
     *[your street address]*
2    *[your city, state and zip]*
     *[your phone number, including area code]*
3
     Petitioner In Pro Per
4

5

6

7

8                          SUPERIOR COURT OF CALIFORNIA

9              COUNTY OF   *[COUNTY in caps, followed by branch name, if any]*

10

11   In the matter of the application of:   )  Case No. *[Case No.]*
                                            )
12   *[NAME OF APPLICANT(S) in caps;*        )  APPLICATION AND ORDER FOR
     *indicate if applicant is a minor]*     )  PUBLICATION RE: CHANGE OF NAME
13   _____   )

14       Application is hereby made for an order directing service of the *["Order to*

15   *Show Cause" or "Notice of Hearing," depending on local rules]* by publication in *[name of*

16   *newspaper]*, which is a newspaper of general circulation in this state most

17   likely to give *[full name of other parent]* notice of the pendency of this proceeding.

18       The whereabouts of *[full name of other parent]* are unknown to the Petitioner.

19   Attempts to locate *[him/her]* are set out in detail in the Due Diligence

20   Declaration(s) filed in support of this application. Petitioner requests that

21   the court issue its order directing service of the *["Order to Show Cause" or "Notice of*

22   *Hearing," depending on local rules]* on *[full name of other parent]* by publication in *[name of*

23   *newspaper]* once a week for four successive weeks as provided in Section 415.50

24   of the Code of Civil Procedure.

25   Dated:  *[today's date]*

26                                       _____

27                                          *[your name]*

28

                                    -1-

**Form 1 — Proof of Service by Mail**

1  [YOUR NAME in caps]
2  [your street address]
   [your city, state and zip]
   [your phone number, including area code]
3  
4  Petitioner In Pro Per
5  
6  
7  
8  SUPERIOR COURT OF CALIFORNIA
9  COUNTY OF [COUNTY in caps, followed by branch name, if any]
10  
11  In the matter of the application of:  )  Case No. [Case No.]
12  [NAME OF APPLICANT(S) in caps:  )  PROOF OF SERVICE BY MAIL
    indicate if applicant is a minor]  )
13  
14  I declare that:
15  1. I am at least 18 years of age and not a party to this legal action.
16  1. My business or residence address is: [Specify address].
17  2. On [date documents were mailed] I served copies of the ["Order to Show Cause" or
18  "Notice of Hearing," depending on local rules] by placing a true and correct copy in a
19  sealed envelope with first-class postage fully prepaid, in the United States
20  mail at [city and state where mailing occurred], addressed as follows: [Specify other parent's
21  full name and address to which documents were mailed].
22  3. I declare under penalty of perjury under the laws of the State of
23  California that the foregoing is true and correct.
24  Dated: [today's date]
25  
26  
27  _____
28  [name of person who served papers]

**Form 2 — Declaration Re: Inability to Ascertain Address**

1  [YOUR NAME in caps]
2  [your street address]
   [your city, state and zip]
   [your phone number, including area code]
3  
4  Petitioner In Pro Per
5  
6  
7  
8  SUPERIOR COURT OF CALIFORNIA
9  COUNTY OF [COUNTY in caps, followed by branch name, if any]
10  
11  In the matter of the application of:  )  Case No. [Case No.]
12  [NAME OF APPLICANT(S) in caps:  )  DECLARATION RE: INABILITY TO
    indicate if applicant is a minor]  )  ASCERTAIN ADDRESS
13  
14  I declare that:
15  1. I am the Petitioner in this legal action.
16  2. On [date judge signed Order for Publication] an order was signed by this court
17  directing that [other parent's full name] be served with the ["Order to Show Cause" or Notice
18  of "Hearing," depending on order] by publication in [name of newspaper].
19  3. I have been unable to ascertain the address of [other parent's full name].
20  Attempts to locate [him/her] are set out in detail in the Due Diligence
21  Declaration(s) filed ["previously" or "along with this declaration"].
22  4. I declare under penalty of perjury under the laws of the State of
23  California that the foregoing is true and correct.
24  Dated: [today's date]
25  
26  _____
27  [your name]
28

## K.  CALL COURT CLERK

IF ALL YOUR PAPERWORK is in order, there's a good chance you can get your name changed without having to appear before a judge, unless the court routinely requires hearings or someone files written objections to (Code of Civil Procedure §1278). A day or two before the scheduled hearing date, call the court clerk. Explain that you have filed a name change petition and give the case number and scheduled hearing date. Then find out:

- whether any written objections have been filed;
- whether you will need to attend the hearing; and
- if the petition was granted without a hearing, how you may obtain certified copies of the Decree Changing Name.

If a hearing is required, make sure you know where and when it will be held.[9]

## L.  APPEAR IN COURT IF REQUIRED

SKIP THIS SECTION if a court appearance is not required. If you are required to attend a hearing, bring with you:

- Copies of all documents you've filed, as well as a copy of the Affidavit of Publication, if the newspaper sent you a copy. Although the judge will have the originals, it's a good idea to bring along copies just in case.
- Several extra copies of the Decree Changing Name.

---

[9]If you can't make the scheduled hearing, you may be able to arrange for a "continuance"—meaning a rescheduling of your hearing at another time or date. Courts have different procedures for arranging continuances. For example, you may need to send a letter to the court confirming the new date. You may need to formally notify anyone who has filed objections or notify the other parent, if the name change is for a child. It's even possible that you'll have to bring a formal motion. If so, see Chapter 9 for information on doing your own research.

- For the name change of a child, it is best to have both parents present, although not required. Children need not attend unless required by local rules. But it is often a good idea, especially if they are older and have opinions about the name change.
- For those petitioning to change a child's name without the consent of the other parent, copies of any final divorce decree and modification of support documents. Also prepare and bring a written record showing the dates of the other parent's support payments and visits to the child.
- If you are a married woman returning to your birth or former name, you may wish to have your husband in the courtroom to show his implicit agreement with your decision. However, that is not legally required.

On the day of the hearing, plan to arrive at the courthouse about half an hour before your scheduled hearing. There will be others scheduled for the same time as you, so don't worry if you are not called right away. You can check with the clerk or bailiff or on the bulletin board to see where you are placed on the schedule.

Sit down and watch some of the cases ahead of you, and get a feel for the procedure. Above all, don't be intimidated by all those lawyers milling around. You should have no problem handling this hearing on your own.

### 1.  Uncontested Case

Many courts do not require a court appearance unless objections were filed to the proposed name change. But local rules vary, and sometimes judges want a personal appearance. Bear in mind that the judge must grant your request unless there is a good reason for denial, so you shouldn't need to convince the judge of anything. Here's the sequence of events.

You are sitting in the courtroom and the bailiff calls the name of your case. You are asked to step forward in front of the judge or on the witness stand to be sworn in ("to tell the truth," etc.). In large counties, judges are not used for routine cases, so you might be asked to "stipulate" (agree) for your case to be heard by a commissioner. For purposes of a name change, a commissioner has the same authority as a judge. Say "Yes."

The judge asks you a few questions to become better informed. Call the judge "Your Honor," and answer her questions briefly. There's no need to volunteer information that is not asked for. Judges are generally helpful to people acting as their own attorneys for name changes. Feel free to ask the judge to explain any questions you don't understand. When the judge is satisfied that the name change should be allowed, she says "granted," and signs the Decree Changing Name. You say, "Thank you, Your Honor" and step down.

Check with the courtroom clerk about how you can get certified copies of the Decree Changing Name. In some counties this can be done right away by having the courtroom clerk initial the copies and then going over to the clerk's office to pay a certification fee and have them stamped.

## 2.  Contested Case

If anyone files written objections to your name change, you'll need to appear in court. You should receive a copy of the written objections at the mailing address you put on your petition. But if you don't receive a copy, go to the clerk's office at the courthouse and ask to see your file. You may also ask for a duplicate copy of the objections for a small photocopying fee.

Written opposition to your petition must state a specific reason for the objection to the name change. Objections can be filed by anyone, but typically they are from:

- a relative who does not approve of the name change, such as a natural father who doesn't want his child's name changed to the stepparent's last name or mother's birth name;

- a prominent person with a name similar to your proposed name who accuses you of wanting to impersonate her or capitalize on her name; or
- a creditor who suspects that you want to change your name to try to avoid paying your debts.

If you face a contested name change, you may wish to arrange for a lawyer to represent you. If so, make sure to emphasize that you've already done all the paperwork and simply want to be represented at the hearing. This shouldn't involve more than an hour or two's work and the fee should be modest. (See Chapter 9, Section B.)

However, you may well want to represent yourself, especially if the written objection isn't substantial and easily can be countered. For example, if someone with a name similar to your new name objects, be prepared to give your legitimate reason for the change. This might be that the new name you've chosen is similar only by coincidence. Be prepared to explain how you decided on the name—maybe it was your uncle's name, or your sister has called you by this nickname since birth.

A contested case proceeds pretty much the same way as an uncontested case—see Section L1 above. You will be sworn in to tell the truth. You might testify from the witness stand, just as if you were a witness at a regular trial. The judge may have you state your reasons for the name change and answer any objections. In some situations, the person opposing the name change will be allowed to voice objections. Always call the judge "Your Honor."

*Example:* Kristophos Yukabonkerzkapowpolis (we'll call him "Kris") files a petition to change his name to Kris Kapow. Unfortunately for Kris, two written objections are filed, one by Cruz Creditor, to whom Kris owes $3,000, and another by Chris Capow, a famous Hollywood stuntwoman who specializes in being shot out of cannons. Cruz thinks Kris wants to use his new name to avoid repaying the money, and Chris is afraid Kris will try to profit from his similar-sounding new name. Here's what Kris says upon being sworn in and taking the witness stand.

*"Good morning, Your Honor. My name is Kris Kapow, and I am petitioning the court to approve my use of this new name, from my former name, Kristophos Yukabonkerzkapowpolis. I want to change my name because my present last name is obviously very difficult to pronounce and spell.*

*"I do not propose this new name in order to avoid any debts, including the one to Mr. Creditor. I am fully aware that a name change has no effect on my debts. I even notified Mr. Creditor a few weeks before filing the petition that he was to use my new adopted name on all correspondence to me. I fully intend to pay him.*

*"As to Ms. Capow's objection, I never intended to use my last name to profit from her identical-sounding last name. In fact, before she filed her objection, I had never heard of her. My own occupation as a professional football player is quite different from hers. I chose the new name "Kapow" because that word is contained in my much longer birth name, and out of ancestral pride I wish to retain a small part of that name."*

After hearing your reasons and any objections, the judge may grant the change right there or decide to think about it (take the matter "under advisement"). If so, you'll be notified by mail or will need to call the clerk and find out the decision. Either way, if the judge grants your petition—which she probably will—you'll need to arrange to get certified copies of the Decree Changing Name.

## M. OBTAIN CERTIFIED COPIES OF DECREE CHANGING NAME

OBTAIN AT LEAST TWO certified copies of the Decree Changing Name from the clerk. This can usually be done right after your court appearance or within a few days of the scheduled hearing date if no appearance is necessary. If the decree is mailed to you after the hearing, it won't be certified unless you've already paid the fee—so you'll still need to obtain certified copies

The cost for certification of a Decree Changing Name is about $2.25 per copy, unless court costs were waived. Check with the court clerk to find out the exact cost and how you can go about getting certified copies. Then either visit the court or submit a self-addressed, stamped envelope and appropriate fees along with your request.

## N. SEND CERTIFIED DECREE TO SECRETARY OF STATE

THE LAST STEP TO MAKE a Court Petition name change valid is to send a certified copy of the Decree Changing Name to the California Secretary of State for the state's records. This must be done within 30 days of the date the judge signs the decree.

Mail one certified Decree Changing Name along with a filing fee ($10.00 currently, but in case fees have gone up, you can send a signed, blank check payable to the Secretary of State with the words "not to exceed $15.00" written on the face) to:

> Secretary of State
> 923 - 12th Street, Suite 301
> Sacramento, California 95814

The telephone number for the Secretary of State division that handles name change notices is (916) 324-6778.

## O. CHANGING BIRTH CERTIFICATE RECORDS

IF YOU WANT TO HAVE a birth certificate amended or a new one issued, read and follow the instructions contained in Chapter 5.

## P. NOTIFY AGENCIES AND INSTITUTIONS

IF NO ONE KNOWS about the name change, it obviously won't do you any good. Turn to Chapter 8 for information on how to notify people of your new name.

# CHAPTER 7

## USAGE METHOD

ALL ADULTS IN CALIFORNIA have the legal right to change their names simply by using the desired new name. There is no need to go to court, and the Usage method costs nothing. To change a name by Usage, the new name must be used consistently, in all aspects of one's business, personal and social life. Children cannot change their names by the Usage method.

## A. NOTIFY AGENCIES AND INSTITUTIONS

LETTING EVERYONE KNOW about your name change is particularly important with a Usage method change. Once you get a few documents with your new name—such as a driver's license and Social Security card—it becomes easier to get the name accepted. Chapter 8 gives information on how to notify people of your new name.

## B. USAGE METHOD DOCUMENTATION

A USAGE METHOD NAME CHANGE does not documentation, but it is advisable to prepare written evidence of the change because:
- You may find it helpful to have a written statement for agencies and businesses. They may be somewhat resistant to your new name, and often you must deal with someone who is not allowed to take your word for anything.

- Sometime in the future, you may need documentation showing when your Usage name change went into effect. For example, after changing your name by Usage, you must wait five years before you can get a passport in the new name.

Copies of the official-looking forms provided in this section are located in Appendix 1. Complete the appropriate form using the accompanying samples as guides. Sign the document in front of a notary public. You can locate one in the Yellow Pages, or through many banks and real estate offices. Notaries usually charge no more than $5.00 to notarize a document.

## 1.  Declaration of Legal Name Change

The Declaration of Legal Name Change officially states that you have changed to a new name.

---

### DECLARATION OF LEGAL NAME CHANGE

I, the undersigned, declare that I am 18 years of age or older and further declare:

1. I, _____[name presently used]_____ , was born _____[name on birth certificate]_____

_____

in __[county where born]__ County in the State of [state where born] on ____[birthdate, year]____ .

2. I HEREBY DECLARE my intent to change my legal name, and be henceforth exclusively known as 3. I further declare that I have no intention of defrauding any person or escaping any obligation I may presently have by this act.

_____[new name]_____

3. I further declare that I have no intention of defrauding any person or escaping any obligation I may presently have by this act.

4. NOTICE IS HEREBY GIVEN to all agencies of the State of California, all agencies of the Federal Government, all creditors and all private persons, groups, businesses, corporations and associations of said legal name change.

I declare under penalty of perjury under the laws of the State of California that the foregoing is true and correct.

Dated: _____      _____
                                              **(new signature)**

                                _____
                                              **(old signature)**

### NOTARIZATION

State of California

County of _____ } SS

On this _____ day of _____ , 19_____ , before me, _____
_____ , a notary public of the State of California, personally
appeared _____ , personally known to me (or proved to me on the
basis of satisfactory evidence) to be the person(s) whose name(s) is/are susbscribed to the within instrument,
and acknowledged to me that she/he/they executed the same in her/his/their authorized capacity(ies), and that
by her/his/their signature(s) on the instrument the person(s), or the entity upon behalf of which the person(s)
acted, executed the instrument.

WITNESS my hand and official seal.      _____

[Notary Seal]                           Signature of Notary Public
                                        Notary Public for the State of California
                                        My commission expires: _____ , 19____

## 2.  Declaration Restoring Former Legal Name

IF YOU WISH TO RETURN to a former name—perhaps because you were divorced or had your marriage annulled some time ago, or simply because you prefer a name you've used previously—use the Declaration Restoring Legal Name.

---

### DECLARATION RESTORING FORMER LEGAL NAME

I, the undersigned, declare that I am 18 years of age or older and further declare:

1. The name I am presently using is _____ **[name presently used]** _____ .

2. My marital status is as follows *(optional)*:

    a. ☐  I was legally divorced in the State of _____ **[state in which divorce occurred]** _____ on **[date of decree, including year]** .

    b. ☐  My marriage was legally annulled in the State of _____ **[state in which annulment occurred]** _____ on **[date of decree, including year]** .

    c. ☐  I am legally married.

    d. ☐  I am single.

3. I HEREBY DECLARE my intent to return to my former legal name, and be henceforth exclusively known as _____ **[former legal name]** _____ .

4. I have no intention of defrauding any person or escaping any obligation I may presently have by this act.

5. NOTICE IS HEREBY GIVEN to all agencies of the State of California, all agencies of the Federal Government, all creditors and all private persons, groups, businesses, corporations and associations of said legal name change.

I declare under penalty of perjury under the laws of the State of California that the foregoing is true and correct.

Dated: _____        _____
                                          (new signature)

                                          _____
                                          (old signature)

### NOTARIZATION

State of California
County of _____ } ss

On this _____ day of _____, 19____, before me, _____
_____, a notary public of the State of California, personally appeared
_____, personally known to me (or proved to me on the basis of satisfactory evidence) to be the person(s) whose name(s) is/are subscribed to the within instrument, and acknowledged to me that she/he/they executed the same in her/his/their authorized capacity(ies), and that by her/his/their signature(s) on the instrument the person(s), or the entity upon behalf of which the person(s) acted, executed the instrument.

WITNESS my hand and official seal.        _____

                                          Signature of Notary Public

[Notary Seal]        Notary Public for the State of California

                                          My commission expires: _____, 19_____

# CHAPTER 8

## HOW TO GET YOUR NEW NAME ACCEPTED

WHETHER YOU HAVE changed your name by Usage or the Court Petition method, the most important part of accomplishing your name change is to let others know you're going by a new name. Although it may take a little time to contact government agencies and businesses, don't be intimidated by the task—it's a common procedure. For example, women who take their husbands' name when they marry do essentially the same thing.

The practical steps to implement a name change are:

- *Advise Officials and Businesses:* Contact the various government and business agencies with which you deal and have your name changed on their records.
- *Enlist Help of Family and Friends:* Tell your friends and family that you have changed your name and that you now want them to use only your new one. The change won't be accomplished overnight. It may take those close to you a while to get used to associating you with a new sound. Some of them might even object to using the new name, perhaps fearing the person they know so well is becoming someone else.
- *Use Only New Name:* If you are employed or in school, go by your new name there. Introduce yourself to new acquaintances and business contacts with your new name.

## A. DOCUMENTATION

WHEN YOU GO TO obtain new identification, it is helpful to take along identification in your old name, as well as documentation that reflects the change to your new name.

If you changed your name using the Court Petition method, you'll simply need to show a certified copy of the Decree Changing Name to agencies and institutions that require proof of your name change. If any insist on keeping a certified copy, you may need to obtain new certified copies of the Decree Changing Name from the court. Contact the court clerk to find out the procedure and cost to obtain additional certified copies.

If you changed your name by the Usage method, you may find it helpful to provide a copy of the official-looking Declaration of Legal Name Change or Declaration Restoring Former Legal Name provided in Chapter 7, Section B.

## B. HOW TO CHANGE IDENTIFICATION AND RECORDS

IT'S GENERALLY RECOMMENDED that you first acquire a driver's license, then obtain a Social Security card in your new name. Once you have those pieces of identification, it's usually no problem to acquire others or have records changed to reflect your name change.

The following chart gives information about how to deal with a variety of agencies to obtain identification or have records changed to reflect your new name.

**Note:** If your name was changed by marriage or any court order such as a divorce or adoption

decree, follow the chart's instructions for the Court Petition method rather than the Usage method. Provide certified copies of the relevant legal documents.

| | COURT PETITION METHOD | USAGE METHOD |
|---|---|---|
| **Driver's License or California ID Card** | Go to the local Department of Motor Vehicles and say that you have changed your name and want the new name on your driver's license or California ID card. You will need to complete and sign a short application (Form DL-44). Check the box on the form entitled "Name Change," provide information about your old license or California ID card and pay the required fee. You will be photographed and the new identification mailed to you.<br><br>If you do not currently have a driver's license or ID card, you'll need to bring along an original or certified copy of your birth certificate, even though your new name will differ from the one on your birth certificate. If you weren't born in the U.S., you'll also need proof that you're legally in the country, such as a green card or naturalization papers (Vehicle Code Section 12801.5, effective 3/94). | Same |
| **Social Security** | Contact your local Social Security office or call (800) 772-1213. Complete and return an Application for a Social Security Number Card (Form SS-5). There is no charge.<br><br>If you already have a Social Security number, use this form to change your name, but don't request a new Social Security number. You must provide a certified copy of the Decree Changing Name. You will probably need to show one additional piece of identification. Acceptable forms of identification are listed in the Usage method column at the right.<br><br>If you are applying for a Social Security number for the first time, you'll also need a certified copy of your birth certificate.<br><br>**Note:** A few Social Security offices have been known to hassle people trying to change their names by | Same, but instead of the court order, you'll need two pieces of identification. One must be in your old name, and one in your new name.<br><br>Acceptable forms of identification include original or certified copies of your:<br><br>• driver's license;<br><br>• U.S. government or state employee ID card;<br><br>• passport;<br><br>• school ID card, record or report card; |

|  | COURT PETITION METHOD | USAGE METHOD |
|---|---|---|
| **Social Security (cont'd)** | refusing to recognize their new names. If you have problems, remind the clerks that they are required to recognize your change of name if you produce "corroborative evidence" as explained in Title 20 of the Code of Federal Regulations §§422.107(c) and 422.110. | • marriage, divorce or adoption records;<br><br>• health insurance card or records from a clinic, doctor or hospital;<br><br>• military records;<br><br>• church membership or confirmation record (this can't be used to establish your age); or<br><br>• insurance policy. |
| **Federal Income Tax** | Since you will be using your new name with everyone, make arrangements for your paychecks, withholding and W-2 forms to be in your new name.<br><br>The SS-5 form filled out for Social Security is automatically forwarded to the Internal Revenue Service, so you are not required to separately contact the IRS about your name change. Simply file your next income tax return using your new name and old social security number. You may file in your new name even if your W-2 is still in in your old name.<br><br>A married couple can file a joint income tax form using two different names. Just write your new name(s) on the form. As of 1989, there is space on the tax forms for each spouse's last name.<br><br>Self-employed married women who kept their birth names may not have had all self-employment taxes correctly credited to them. Until 1989, joint tax returns had no room for *both* spouse's last names, and self-employment taxes were routinely reported under the husband's name. If the wife's name was different, she wasn't given the appropriate credit—meaning her future benefits could be reduced. Although women in this situation should have been contacted by the Social Security Administration or IRS, not everyone was. To verify that you received credit for all self-employment taxes paid, contact your local Social Security office or call (800) 772-1213. To get a record of your income, obtain a Request for Earnings and Benefit Estimate Statement (Form SSA-7004-PC-OP2). | Same |

|  | COURT PETITION METHOD | USAGE METHOD |
|---|---|---|
| **State Income Tax** | Send a letter to Taxpayer Services, Franchise Tax Board, P.O. Box 942840, Sacramento, California 94240-0000. Say that you have changed your name and give your old name, new name and Social Security number. Use your new name and old Social Security number when filing any later tax returns or forms. | Same |
| **Voting** | Register under your new name by completing an Affidavit of Voter Registration, usually available at libraries, post offices and other public buildings. If you have been registered to vote before, you will need to state the name, address and political party listed in your most recent registration. Take or mail the completed form to the county Registrar of Voters. Once you've registered, you can vote and sign petitions using your new name. | Same |
| **Passports** | If you already have a U.S. passport, you must provide a certified copy of the Decree Changing Name. You have two choices:<br><br>**Amend Passport.** You can have your current passport amended to reflect both your old and new names. There is no charge, and you can send in the application by mail. Use Passport Amendment/Validation Application (Form DSP-19).<br><br>**Obtain New Passport.** You can get a new passport that shows only your new name. If you apply at a passport office, use Passport Application (Form DSP-11) and pay the appropriate fee. If you have been issued a U.S. passport within the last twelve years, you can apply by mail and pay a smaller fee using Application for Passport By Mail (Form DSP-82).<br><br>If you have not been issued a U.S. passport within the last twelve years, you must apply in person. Use Passport Application (Form DSP-11) and pay the fee. You must also provide proof of citizenship such as a certified copy of your birth certificate, as well as a certified copy of the Decree Changing Name and a piece of identification with your new name and signature—such as a driver's license or photo ID from your work, the military or U.S. government. | To obtain a passport issued in a name changed by the Usage method, you must have used the new name for at least five years unless:<br><br>• You're willing to retain your old name in the passport and have the new name added as an AKA ("also known as");<br><br>• The new name is similar to the old—for example, the name change consists of transposing first and middle names, making minor spelling changes, adding or deleting a first or middle name, adopting a common nickname or Americanizing a foreign first or middle name;<br><br>• You are a married, divorced or widowed woman using your birth or previous married name exclusively; or |

| | COURT PETITION METHOD | USAGE METHOD |
|---|---|---|
| **Passports (cont'd)** | Obtain copies of applications by contacting an office that handles passports. They are located in post offices or county clerk's offices. Or contact:<br><br>Los Angeles Passport Agency<br>Federal Building, Room 13100<br>11000 Wilshire Boulevard<br>Los Angeles, CA 90024-3615<br><br>San Francisco Passport Agency<br>525 Market Street, Room 200<br>San Francisco, CA 94105-2773 | • Your name was not recorded at birth, was recorded incorrectly or was changed during childhood.<br><br>You'll need identification in your new name, such as a driver's license or photo ID from your work, the military or U.S. government. You might need special affidavits from your relatives or others who know about the change.<br><br>If you changed your name more than five years ago, you may obtain a passport issued exclusively in your new name. You'll need identification in your new name, documents substantiating how long you've been using it and special affidavits from people able to confirm when you began using the new name.<br><br>Exact documentation requirements vary depending on your situation and the reason for the name change. Contact an office that handles passport applications listed in the Court Petition method section at the left.<br><br>If a child is known by her stepfather's last name, a passport may sometimes be issued in that name, even though a legal adoption has not taken place. This requires the written consent of the natural father or a special affidavit by the mother indicating that the natural father is dead or his whereabouts are unknown. |

|  | COURT PETITION METHOD | USAGE METHOD |
|---|---|---|
| **Bank Accounts** | Go to the bank where you have an account and provide a certified copy of the Decree Changing Name. Most banks will insist on seeing a piece of identification with your new name, such as a driver's license or other photo ID. You will need to sign a new signature card, and probably re-do all prior documentationto reflect your name change. Banks will probably cross-list you in their records under both your new and old names. If you expect to receive checks made payable to your old name, advise the bank officer and make sure you are listed under both names. Remember to order checks with your new name. | Same, with the exception that you will not provide a copy of the court order. |
| **Credit Cards** | Notify your credit card companies of the change and request new cards. To protect your credit history, make sure that the original date of the account is included along with your new name.<br><br>California law provides that no business may refuse to do business with a woman because she uses her birth or former name, regardless of her marital status (Code of Civil Procedure §1279.6). Credit card companies are required by law to issue credit cards in a woman's birth or married name—the choice of name is entirely up to her. However, the credit card company may insist that a married woman establish an account separate from her husband's (Civil Code §1747.81).<br><br>If you have previously been known by your married name, your credit records may be only in your husband's name and may not reflect your credit history. To ensure that you have a credit history in your own name, write to your credit card company and make sure they report your new name with the original opening date of the joint account.<br><br>**Resource:** For more information about women and credit, you may want to obtain the pamphlet "Women's Credit Rights," put out by Bankcard Holders of America, 560 Herndon Parkway, Suite 120, Herndon, VA 22070. Similar publications are available from the Washington, D.C. based Federal Trade Commission and Federal Deposit Insurance Corporation's Office of Consumer Affairs. | Same |

|  | COURT PETITION METHOD | USAGE METHOD |
|---|---|---|
| **Public Assistance (Welfare)** | Take a certified copy of the Decree Changing Name to your local welfare office. They will change their records so you will receive payments under your new name.<br><br>When you complete your monthly reporting statement, indicate that you have changed your name. You can fill in the information in the section that asks whether you have anything else to report. | Same, but simply tell the local welfare office you have changed your name and give your new name. |
| **Birth Certificates and Attachments** | See Chapter 5, Section A for information about when you can get a completely new California birth certificate issued reflecting a new name.<br><br>If you are not eligible for a completely new California birth certificate, you are entitled to add an official attachment if you provide a certified copy of the Decree Changing Name and pay the appropriate fee, as described in Chapter 5, Section B.<br><br>Information on California birth certificates and details about when they can be amended or reissued is covered in Chapter 5. If you were born outside of California, check with the vital statistics office in the state or country of your birth. | No new California birth certificates or official attachments can be obtained for Usage method name changes. However, an official attachment reflecting a parent's new name may be added to a child's birth certificate, as discussed in Chapter 5, Section B.<br><br>See Chapter 5 for more information on when you may be entitled to obtain a new or amended birth certificate. |
| **Stocks, Bonds, Mutual Funds, Vehicles and Other Assets With Title** | Contact the title company, business or financial institution that is holding the assets and arrange to have title changed to reflect your new name. You may choose to write a letter stating that you, *[Former Name]*, have changed your name to *[New Name]*.<br><br>**Stocks and Bonds:** Complete any transfer documents required. You will probably need to send the stock or bond certificate along with a signed letter to the transfer agent listed on the certificate. Make a photocopy of the certificate in case the original is lost in the mail. You will receive a certificate in your new name.<br><br>**Vehicles:** To have a vehicle re-registered in your new name, go to the Department of Motor Vehicles. Complete and file a Name Change Statement (Form 597), for which there is no charge. To change the title (pink slip), you must be the full legal owner. Or you must contact the institution that holds the title and request that it initiate the name change. This usually isn't necessary until you're ready to sell the vehicle. | Same |

| | COURT PETITION METHOD | USAGE METHOD |
|---|---|---|
| **Deeds** | If you own real estate, you should change the deed to reflect your new name. This will avoid confusion if you sell or refinance your property. It also will show you did not change your name with the intent of defrauding anyone. You must list both your former and new names on the deed when you sell your property (Civil Code §1096).<br><br>Here is how to change your deed. Go to a stationery store or a title company and pick up a blank deed that corresponds to your deed (usually a "grant" deed). Draw up a new deed following the basic form of your old deed but transferring the property from your former name to your new name. Use wording such as: "*[New Name]*, who acquired title under the former name of *[Former Name]* hereby grants to *[New Name]* the following property:" Then include the full legal description of the property.<br><br>Above the main part of the deed, there will be a section on transfer tax. If available, check the box before words such as "This transfer is exempt from the documentary transfer tax." Or type in the words, "no valuable consideration."<br><br>Sign the deed in your new name and have it notarized. Complete a Preliminary Change of Ownership Report, available from the county recorder or county assessor. Where the form requires transfer information, indicate that the transaction is only a correction of the name on the deed.<br><br>Finally, record your deed with the county recorder's office and pay the appropriate fee. Current fees are about $5.00 for the first page and $2.00 for each additional page.<br><br>**Resource:** Detailed information about deeds and step-by-step instructions on preparing deed forms can be found in *The Deeds Book: How to Transfer Title to California Real Estate* by Mary Randolph (Nolo Press). | Same |
| **Mortgages** | Notify the mortgage company of your new name. There is no change in your liability for the mortgage. | Same |

|  | COURT PETITION METHOD | USAGE METHOD |
|---|---|---|
| **Wills, Estate Planning and Inheritances** | Don't worry—you won't lose your inheritance by changing your name. If you are listed on someone's will in your old name or stand to receive a family inheritance, you still will be entitled to it. You could ask your benefactor to revise her will, but it isn't necessary. For example, a woman who changes her name by marriage does not lose any inheritance listed in her birth name. To avoid any confusion, when someone dies who might have left you an inheritance, notify the executor or administrator of the estate of your old and new names.<br><br>If you have your own will or other estate planning documents (such as a living trust), it is best to replace them with new documents reflecting your new name. Again, your relatives will not lose their inheritances just because you change your name. | Same |
| **Insurance** | Let your insurance carrier know of your name change. Have policies reissued in your new name.<br><br>**Automobile Insurance:** Notify your agent of the name change. Auto insurance rates are not affected by name changes.<br><br>**Health Insurance:** Notify the insurance carrier of the change. If you have coverage through your spouse's employer, she may have to sign a form requesting that a card be issued in your name under the same coverage.<br><br>**Life Insurance:** Notify the company of the name change if you hold a policy or are the beneficiary of a policy. Should you neglect to notify a company of the name change, it won't alter your right to receive insurance proceeds. | Same |
| **Creditors and Debtors** | Changing your name does not make your debts disappear. Notify your creditors about the change, including holders of promissory notes, medical and legal professionals, landlords and anyone who obtained a court judgment against you.<br><br>You'll need to contact anyone who owes you money, such as renters or debtors against whom you obtained a court judgment. Notify them of your new name and ask that payments be made in your new name. Changing your name does not affect their debt to you. | Same |

|  | COURT PETITION METHOD | USAGE METHOD |
|---|---|---|
| **Post Office** | List both your old and new name on your mailbox, so the carrier will know to deliver mail addressed to you in either name. Eventually, you should receive all mail in your new name and may then want to remove your old name from the mailbox. | Same |
| **Telephone and Utilities** | Contact the telephone company and advise them of the name change. If you want to be listed in the directory under both old and new names, there will be a set-up charge (approximately $5.00) and a minimal monthly charge. Or you could be listed only in your new name.<br><br>Contact your local utility companies and advise them of the name change. If you change both your first and last names, you may have problems with local utilities, especially if they require a deposit for new customers. Let them know you've changed your name but are the same person, and can provide them with documentation to that effect. You may then need to send a copy of the Decree Changing Name. | Same, but if documentation is required, you can use a name change declaration presented in Chapter 7, Section B. |
| **School Records** | Have your schools change your name on their records in case an employer sends for copies of your grades. (Sunday schools are optional.) You can also petition the school to have your diploma reissued in your new name. | Same |
| **Veterans Administration** | Contact the local VA office and let them know you have changed your name. Some offices will accept a letter signed in your new name. Or you can fill in Form 21-4138, a blank form put out by the VA. Sending a certified copy of the Decree Changing Name would be helpful. | Same, but if documentation is required, you can use a name change declaration presented in Chapter 7, Section B. |
| **Employer's Records** | Let your employer know you only want to be called by your new name. Have your name changed in your employment records, including payroll and tax records. If you work as an independent contractor, give your customers your new name. | Same |
| **Legal and Other Important Documents** | All important papers should be revised to reflect your new name. This includes legal documents such as durable or regular powers of attorney, living wills, trusts and contracts. | Same |

|  | COURT PETITION METHOD | USAGE METHOD |
|---|---|---|
| **Other Records** | Look through your correspondence, address book, the contents of your wallet and your important papers to discover if there are other people, businesses or agencies you must contact. Write a short letter stating that you have legally changed your name and want only your new name to be used from now on. No documentation is needed. | Same |

## C. PROBLEMS GETTING NEW NAME ACCEPTED

Agencies should accept your name change without hassle. However, some agencies, particularly schools, may be reluctant to accept a Usage method name change. Start by providing documentation that shows both the old and new names. For Usage method name changes made within the last five years, a passport may be helpful since it can show the old name as well as the new name as an AKA ("also know as").

If you have problems, you may want to gently but forcefully give a rundown of California law that supports your position (see sidebar). If you run into an uncooperative clerk, ask to speak to his supervisor. Be confident that you have the legal right to change your name, even if the people you're dealing with don't know your rights. Keep going up the ladder until you get results. If you have trouble at the local office of a government agency, contact the main office. If you come up against a seemingly impossible situation, get the help of your local elected official.

---

### California Law Supports
### Usage Method Name Change

California adults may effect a legal name change without going to court. This is supported by Code of Civil Procedure §1279.5; *Cabrera v. McMullen* (1988) 204 Cal. App. 3d 1; *In re Ritchie* (1984) 159 Cal. App. 3d 1070; *In re Banks Marriage* (1974) 42 Cal. App. 3d 631; *Sousa v. Freitas* (1970) 10 Cal. App. 3d 660; *Application of Trower* (1968) 260 Cal. App. 2d 75.

# CHAPTER 9

## FINDING ADDITIONAL HELP

ALTHOUGH NAME CHANGES are not procedurally difficult, you may want someone to help you complete forms or check over your paperwork. Perhaps you want to do some legal research on matters that are not covered here. Or maybe you need a lawyer to assist you with a contested name change or legal issues that go beyond the scope of this book.

## A. INDEPENDENT PARALEGALS ("TYPING SERVICES")

UNTIL RECENTLY, THOSE who didn't hire a lawyer to help with a legal problem had two choices: they could handle the problem on their own or not handle it at all. Now, though, a number of businesses known as "independent paralegals" or "typing services" have emerged to assist people in filling out legal forms. Simple procedures such as name changes, uncontested divorces and bankruptcies are all routinely handled by independent paralegals at a substantially lower cost than lawyers would charge.

Typing services are very different from lawyers in that they can't give legal advice or represent you in court—by law, only lawyers are allowed to do those things. They can, however:

- Provide instructions and legal information needed to handle your own name change;

- Provide the appropriate forms; and
- Type your papers so they'll be accepted by a court.

As a general matter, the longer a typing service has been in business, the better. People at a typing service should be up front with you about not being attorneys and not providing legal advice. The following statement, posted in a prominent typing service in the Oakland/San Francisco Bay Area, summarizes its services well:

*WE ARE NOT ATTORNEYS.*

*We are pro per assistants. Attorneys represent people. We assist people to represent themselves. If you want someone to represent you, you will need to hire an attorney. If you want to "do it yourself," we can help. We believe that representing yourself is the only way to gain, and keep, control over your own life and your own legal problems. You don't need legal training to use the courts or manage your own legal affairs. You have a constitutional right to represent yourself without an attorney. Let us assist you!*

A recommendation from someone who has used a particular typing service is the best way to find a reputable one in your area. The services

newspapers or in local throwaway papers like the Classified Flea Market or Giant Nickel. They may be listed in the Yellow Pages under "typing services" or "paralegals."

## B. LAWYERS

LAWYERS—ALSO CALLED ATTORNEYS—are the only people allowed to give legal advice in California. Lawyers must be licensed by passing the California bar examination, which tests their knowledge of different areas of law. Almost all lawyers have gone to law school, but a few have followed special self-study courses and passed the bar without attending law school.

Finding a lawyer you trust and who also charges reasonable prices is not always an easy task. It is natural to feel a little intimidated, but it may be helpful to remember that a lawyer is simply someone you hire to do legal work for you. Here are some suggestions for finding and hiring lawyers. We do not recommend one or another source. You may need to check around until you find someone you feel comfortable hiring.

- **Personal Referrals:** If you know someone who was pleased with his lawyer, check with that person. If the lawyer can't take on your case, she might be willing to recommend someone else who is experienced, competent and available.
- **Group Legal Practice:** Some unions, employers and consumer action organizations offer plans to their members or employees for legal work at rates substantially lower than is

available through most private practitioners. If you're a member of such a plan, check with it for a lawyer, especially if your problem is covered for free. However, beware of plans which do no more than refer you to a local attorney who will supposedly give you a good price.

- **Law Clinics:** Law clinics such as Hyatt Legal Services and Jacoby and Meyers loudly advertise their low initial consultation fees. This generally means that a basic consultation is inexpensive—often about $20—but anything beyond that isn't so cheap. If you're comfortable with the lawyer you talk with and the representation, it may be worthwhile to hire him. But be sure that the advertised or quoted price includes everything you think it does.
- **Pre-Paid Legal Insurance:** So-called "legal insurance" plans are marketed by companies such as Bank of America, Montgomery Ward and Amway.[1] These plans often are offered by mail to credit card customers and in some cases are sold door-to-door. Many of these plans offer several free legal consultations, a simple will and some letter writing for a monthly charge of less than $10.00. Of course, there's no guarantee that the lawyers available through these plans are of the best caliber; sometimes they aren't.
- **Lawyer Referral Panels:** Most county bar associations maintain services that will give you the names of some attorneys who practice in your area. Usually, you can get a referral to a lawyer who specializes in the area you need, and an initial consultation for a low fee. A problem with the panels is that they usually provide minimal screening for the attorneys

---

[1]It's a misnomer to refer to these programs as "legal insurance." The programs provide an initial level of service for a low fee and then charge specific fees for additional or different work. Thus, most pre-paid plans are more a marketing device for the participating lawyers than they are an insurance plan. As with any consumer transaction, check out the plan carefully before signing up. A good place to start checking is with your local bar association.

listed, which means those who participate may not be the most experienced or competent. It may be possible to find a skilled attorney willing to work for a reasonable fee following this approach, but take time to check out the credentials and experience of the person to whom you are referred.

- **Yellow Pages:** The Yellow Pages in every telephone book have an extensive number of entries under "Attorneys." They are listed both by specialty and in alphabetical order. Some ads may quote initial consultation rates. If all else fails, let your fingers do the walking.

## C. DOING YOUR OWN LEGAL RESEARCH

EVERY CALIFORNIA COUNTY maintains a law library that is required to serve all members of the public—not just lawyers and judges. Although some libraries have more books than others, all have the California statutes, written court opinions, and expert commentary. In addition, some local public libraries also have quite extensive collections of law and legal research books. Before making a special trip to the law library, you may first want to check with the public library.

### 1. Looking up Citations

This book includes many numbered references to California law. These are called "citations," and most refer to various sets of statutes, such as the Civil Code, Code of Civil Procedure and Health and Safety Code. You may find statutes in a single volume of each code, or in one section of a book which consists of several codes. You usually can find these books in a good-sized public library.

There also are multi-volume annotated book sets which give the statutes and information about each statute. They have information about the history of each statute—when it was first

passed, when different sections were amended, along with citations of cases and very short summaries of cases in which courts interpreted the statute. The case law summaries are by no means complete, so read the case yourself rather than relying on the annotation.

### 2. Looking Up Cases

"Case law" refers to judges' published opinions about a dispute that was resolved in court. These decisions give important information about how a law has been interpreted. If you can find a case decision in which the facts were similar to your situation, you can get some guidance on how a court might decide your case.

A "case citation" is a shorthand identification of the volume, series of volumes and page number where the case can be found. The "official" volumes of cases are published by the California appellate courts as *Official Reports of the California Supreme Court* (abbreviated Cal. or Cal.2d or Cal.3d, representing the first, second and third series of the volumes) and as *Official*

*Reports of the California Courts of Appeal* (abbreviated Cal.App., Cal.App.2d and Cal.App.3d). Cases are also published by the West Publishing Company in "unofficial" volumes—the *California Reporter* (Cal. Rptr.) and *Pacific Reporter* (P. or P.2d). The published case decision will be the same, word for word, whether you read it in the "official" or "unofficial" report.

## 3. Learning Legal Research Techniques

If you want to find the answer to a legal question you have, rather than simply look up a specific statute or case to which you already have the citation, you will need some guidance in basic legal research techniques. An excellent place to start is with *Legal Research: How to Find and Understand the Law* by Stephen Elias (Nolo Press). Additional good resources that may be available in your law library include:

- *Legal Research Made Easy: A Roadmap Through the Law Library Maze,* a 2 1/2 hour video by Nolo Press and Legal Star Communications.

- *The Legal Research Manual: A Game Plan for Legal Research and Analysis* by Christopher and Jill Wren, 2d ed. Madison, WI, A-R Editions, 1986.
- *Introduction to Legal Research: A Layperson's Guide to Finding the Law* by Al Coco, Want Publishing Co., 1985.
- *How to Find the Law* by Morris Cohen and Robert Berring, 8th ed., West Publishing Co., 1983.

The best way to get answers to specific questions is to first locate a good background resource. The topics you will be looking for will probably will be listed in the card catalog under the term "name change" or possibly "change of name." Most background resources contain references to statutes or cases. Once you have a general understanding of an issue, you can read the statutes or cases referred to for a more precise understanding of what the law provides. When you find a statute or case that directly concerns your issue, the next step is to determine whether the statute has been amended or whether a later court case has shed new light on the matter. The legal research resources listed earlier will help you do this.

# GLOSSARY OF NAMES

**BIRTH NAME:** The name originally given to a person and listed on the birth certificate (if there was one). For a married woman who changed her name, this refers to the **Last Name** given at birth.

**FAMILY NAME:** See **Last Name**.

**FIRST NAME:** Examples of first names include Betty, Jack, Fred and Susan.

**FORMER NAME:** A name used previously by someone who has changed his name.

**GIVEN NAME:** See **First Name**.

**LAST NAME:** Examples of last names include Johnson, Perez, Wong and McCoy.

**MAIDEN NAME:** See **Birth Name**.

**MARRIED NAME:** If a woman has changed her name upon marrying, the new **Last Name**, which is generally that of her husband.

**MIDDLE NAME:** A name inbetween a **First Name** and **Last Name**. Some married woman choose to make this either their **Birth Name**, if they adopt their husband's **Last Name**, or their husband's **Last Name**, if they keep their **Birth Name**.

**NICKNAME:** A shortened, familiar or informal name, rarely used for official purposes.

**PRESENT NAME:** The old name you want to change.

**PROPOSED NAME:** The new name by which you want to be known.

**SURNAME:** See **Last Name**.

**APPENDIX 1**

## FORMS FOR NAME CHANGE BY USAGE METHOD

# MARRIAGE SURNAME AGREEMENT
## (Antenuptial Agreement)

This agreement is made between _____

and _____ in consideration of

the contemplated marriage of said parties.

It is hereby agreed between the parties that _____

upon and during the marriage will not assume the surname of _____,

but will retain her own name.

NOTICE IS HEREBY GIVEN to all agencies of the State of California, all agencies of the Federal

Government, all creditors and all private persons, groups, businesses, corporations and associations, that

_____ will retain for all purposes said name upon

and during her marriage to _____.


Dated: _____      _____
                                                    (signature)

Dated: _____      _____
                                                    (signature)

# PARENTAL AGREEMENT ON CHILD'S NAME

This agreement is made between _____ and

_____ in consideration of the contemplated birth

of a child born of said couple.

It is hereby agreed between the parties that the child will be given the _____

name of _____.


Dated: _____        _____

(signature)

Dated: _____        _____

(signature)

# DECLARATION OF LEGAL NAME CHANGE

I, the undersigned, declare that I am 18 years of age or older and further declare:

1. I, _____, was born _____

_____ in

_____ County in the State of _____ on _____.

2. I HEREBY DECLARE my intent to change my legal name, and be henceforth exclusively known as

_____.

3. I further declare that I have no intention of defrauding any person or escaping any obligation I may presently have by this act.

4. NOTICE IS HEREBY GIVEN to all agencies of the State of California, all agencies of the Federal Government, all creditors and all private persons, groups, businesses, corporations and associations of said legal name change.

I declare under penalty of perjury under the laws of the State of California that the foregoing is true and correct.

Dated: _____          _____
                                                          (new signature)

                                        _____
                                                          (old signature)

## NOTARIZATION

State of California

County of _____ } ss

On this _____ day of _____, 19_____, before me, _____

_____, a notary public of the State of California, personally

appeared _____, personally known to me (or proved to me on the basis of satisfactory evidence) to be the person(s) whose name(s) is/are subscribed to the within instrument, and acknowledged to me that she/he/they executed the same in her/his/their authorized capacity(ies), and that by her/his/their signature(s) on the instrument the person(s), or the entity upon behalf of which the person(s) acted, executed the instrument.

WITNESS my hand and official seal.          _____
                                                          Signature of Notary Public

[Notary Seal]                              Notary Public for the State of California

                                        My commission expires: _____, 19____

# DECLARATION RESTORING FORMER LEGAL NAME

I, the undersigned, declare that I am 18 years of age or older and further declare:

1. The name I am presently using is _____.

2. My marital status is as follows *(optional):*

   a. ☐ I was legally divorced in the State of _____ on _____, 19____.

   b. ☐ My marriage was legally annulled in the State of _____ on _____, 19____.

   c. ☐ I am legally married.

   d. ☐ I am single.

3. I HEREBY DECLARE my intent to return to my former legal name, and be henceforth exclusively known as _____.

4. I have no intention of defrauding any person or escaping any obligation I may presently have by this act.

5. NOTICE IS HEREBY GIVEN to all agencies of the State of California, all agencies of the Federal Government, all creditors and all private persons, groups, businesses, corporations and associations of said legal name change.

I declare under penalty of perjury under the laws of the State of California that the foregoing is true and correct.

Dated: _____

_____
(new signature)

_____
(old signature)

## NOTARIZATION

State of California

County of _____ } ss

On this _____ day of _____, 19_____, before me, _____ _____, a notary public of the State of California, personally appeared _____, personally known to me (or proved to me on the basis of satisfactory evidence) to be the person(s) whose name(s) is/are subscribed to the within instrument, and acknowledged to me that she/he/they executed the same in her/his/their authorized capacity(ies), and that by her/his/their signature(s) on the instrument the person(s), or the entity upon behalf of which the person(s) acted, executed the instrument.

WITNESS my hand and official seal.

_____
Signature of Notary Public

[Notary Seal]

Notary Public for the State of California

My commission expires: _____, 19____

# APPENDIX 2

## FORMS FOR NAME CHANGE BY COURT ORDER

<table>
<tr><td>
PARTY WITHOUT AN ATTORNEY (Name and Address):

TELEPHONE NO.:

In Pro Per
</td><td>FOR COURT USE ONLY</td></tr>
</table>

**SUPERIOR COURT OF CALIFORNIA, COUNTY OF:**

STREET ADDRESS:

MAILING ADDRESS:

CITY AND ZIP CODE:

BRANCH NAME:

IN THE MATTER OF THE APPLICATION OF:

| PETITION FOR CHANGE OF NAME | CASE NUMBER: |
|---|---|

1. Petitioner(s) _____

   _____

   request(s) that this court make an order to show cause at a specified time and place why this application for change of name should not be granted, and upon hearing this court make an order changing Applicant(s)' name from

   _____

   _____

   to _____

   _____

2. ☐ There are two or more Applicants. The information requested in Items 3-10 for each additional Applicant is supplied in a separate Attachment 2.

3. Applicant (name): _____

   a. ☐ was born on _____, 19_____ and is over the age of eighteen years.

   b. ☐ is a minor under eighteen years of age, born on _____, 19_____, and is related to the Petitioner(s) as: _____.

4. Applicant's present name is: _____.

5. Applicant's proposed name is: _____.

6. Applicant was born in _____, and presently resides at _____, in the County of _____, State of California.

7. The reason for the proposed name change is:

**PETITION FOR CHANGE OF NAME**

IN THE MATTER OF THE APPLICATION OF:

| | CASE NUMBER: |
|---|---|

8. ☐ Additional facts supporting petition are as follows:

a. ☐ Applicant's father consents to the proposed name change.

b. ☐ Applicant's mother consents to the proposed name change.

c. ☐ Other:

9. The names, residence addresses and relationships of Applicant's relatives so far as known to Petitioner(s) are as follows:

a. ☐ Father: _____

b. ☐ Mother: _____

c. ☐ Applicant's father and mother are deceased. Applicant's near relatives, their relationships and respective residence addresses so far as known to Petitioner(s), are as follows:

10. ☐ (Complete only if Applicant is a minor.) Petitioner(s) request(s) that notice to the following person(s) be dispensed with for the reasons specified in Attachment 10:

a. ☐ Applicant's father (name): _____

b. ☐ Applicant's mother (name): _____

11. ☐ Number of pages attached:

I declare under penalty of perjury under the laws of the State of California that the foregoing is true and correct.

Date:

_____  _____
Signature of Petitioner          Signature of Second Petitioner

_____  _____
(Type or Print Name)             (Type or Print Name)

**ATTACHMENT 2 TO PETITION FOR CHANGE OF NAME: INFORMATION ON ADDITIONAL APPLICANTS**

*(use a separate Attachment for each additional applicant)*

3.  Applicant *(name):* _____

    a. ☐ was born on _____, 19_____ and is over the age of eighteen years.

    b. ☐ is a minor under eighteen years of age, born on _____, 19_____, and is
related to the Petitioner(s) as: _____.

4.  Applicant's present name is: _____.

5.  Applicant's proposed name is: _____.

6.  Applicant was born in _____, and presently resides at
_____, in the
County of _____, State of California.

7.  The reason for the proposed name change is:

8.  ☐ Additional facts supporting petition are as follows:

    a. ☐ Applicant's father consents to the proposed name change.

    b. ☐ Applicant's mother consents to the proposed name change.

    c. ☐ Other:

9.  The names, residence addresses and relationships of Applicant's relatives so far as known to Petitioner(s) are as
follows:

    a. ☐ Father: _____

    b. ☐ Mother: _____

    c. ☐ Applicant's father and mother are deceased. Applicant's near relatives, their relationships and respective
residence addresses so far as known to Petitioner(s), are as follows:

10. ☐ *(Complete only if Applicant is a minor.)* Petitioner(s) request(s) that notice to the following person be dispensed
with for the reasons specified in Attachment 10:

    a. ☐ Applicant's father *(name):* _____

    b. ☐ Applicant's mother *(name):* _____

<table>
<tr><td>PARTY WITHOUT AN ATTORNEY (Name and Address):<br><br><br><br><br>In Pro Per</td><td>TELEPHONE NO.:</td><td>FOR COURT USE ONLY</td></tr>
</table>

**SUPERIOR COURT OF CALIFORNIA, COUNTY OF:**

STREET ADDRESS:

MAILING ADDRESS:

CITY AND ZIP CODE:

BRANCH NAME:

IN THE MATTER OF THE APPLICATION OF:

<table>
<tr><td>**ORDER TO SHOW CAUSE FOR CHANGE OF NAME**<br>☐ **AND ORDER DISPENSING NOTICE**</td><td>CASE NUMBER:</td></tr>
</table>

1.  THE COURT FINDS that Petitioner(s) _____

    _____

    has/have filed a Petition for Change of Name with the clerk of this court for an order changing Applicant(s)' name from

    _____

    _____

    to _____

    _____.

2.  THE COURT ORDERS:

    a.  All people interested in this matter appear before this court to show cause why this application for change of name should not be granted on:

    | Hearing date: | Time: | ☐ Dept.: | ☐ Div.: | ☐ Room: |
    |---|---|---|---|---|

    located at (address of court):

    b.  A copy of this order to show cause be published once a week for four successive weeks prior to the day of said

    hearing in _____, a newspaper of

    general circulation printed in the County of _____.

    c.  ☐  Notice be dispensed with to the following person(s):

        1.  ☐  Applicant's father (name): _____

        2.  ☐  Applicant's mother (name): _____

Dated: ...................................................................        _____

                                                                            (Judge of the Superior Court)

PARTY WITHOUT AN ATTORNEY *(Name and Address)*:

TELEPHONE NO.:

FOR COURT USE ONLY

*In Pro Per*

**SUPERIOR COURT OF CALIFORNIA, COUNTY OF:**

STREET ADDRESS:

MAILING ADDRESS:

CITY AND ZIP CODE:

BRANCH NAME:

IN THE MATTER OF THE APPLICATION OF:

**DECREE  CHANGING  NAME**

CASE NUMBER:

1.  The Petition for Change of Name for an order changing Applicant's name from _____

_____

to _____

came on for hearing as follows:

a.  Judge *(name)*: _____

b.  Hearing date: _____  Time: _____  ☐ Dept.: _____  ☐ Div.: _____  ☐ Room: _____

2.  THE COURT FINDS:

a. ☐  All notices required by law have been given.

b. ☐  No objections were filed by any person.

c. ☐  The allegations of the petition are sufficient and true.

3.  THE COURT ORDERS:

This petition be granted and that the name of Applicant be and is changed from _____

_____

to _____.

Dated: ...................................................    _____

(Judge of the Superior Court)

| ATTORNEY OR PARTY WITHOUT ATTORNEY *(Name and Address)*: | TELEPHONE NO.: | *FOR COURT USE ONLY* |
|---|---|---|
| | | |

ATTORNEY FOR *(Name)*:

| NAME OF COURT: |
| STREET ADDRESS: |
| MAILING ADDRESS: |
| CITY AND ZIP CODE: |
| BRANCH NAME: |

In the matter of the application of:

### APPLICATION FOR
### WAIVER OF COURT FEES AND COSTS

CASE NUMBER:

I request a court order so that I do not have to pay court fees and costs.

1. My address and date of birth are *(specify)*:

2. ☐ I am receiving financial assistance under one or more of the following programs:
   a. ☐ **SSI and SSP:** The Supplemental Security Income and State Supplemental Payments Programs
   b. ☐ **AFDC:** The Aid to Families with Dependent Children Program
   c. ☐ **Food Stamps:** The Food Stamps Program
   d. ☐ **County Relief, General Relief (G.R.) or General Assistance (G.A.)**

*[If you checked box 2 above, sign at the bottom of this side and DO NOT fill out the rest of the form.]*

3. ☐ My gross monthly income is less than the amount shown on the Information Sheet on Waiver of Court Fees and Costs available from the clerk's office.

*[If you checked box 3 above, skip 4, complete 5 and 6 on the back of this form, and sign at the bottom of this side.]*

4. ☐ My income is not enough to pay for the common necessaries of life for me and the people in my family I support and also pay court fees and costs. *[If you checked this box you must complete the back of this form.]*

> WARNING: You must immediately tell the court if you become able to pay court fees or costs during this action. For the next three (3) years you may be ordered to appear in court and answer questions about your ability to pay court fees or costs.

I declare under penalty of perjury under the laws of the State of California that the foregoing is true and correct.

Date:

_____          _____
*(TYPE OR PRINT NAME)*                              *(SIGNATURE)*

Form Adopted by the
Judicial Council of California
982(a)(17) [Rev. January 1, 1985]

**APPLICATION FOR WAIVER OF COURT FEES AND COSTS**
**(In Forma Pauperis)**

Gov. Code,
§ 68511.3

## FINANCIAL INFORMATION

5. ☐ My pay changes considerably from month to month. *[If you check this box, each of the amounts reported in 6 should be your average for the past 12 months.]*

6. My monthly income:

a. My gross monthly pay is: . . . . . . . . . $_____

b. My payroll deductions are *(specify purpose and amount)*:

(1) _____ $_____
(2) _____ $_____
(3) _____ $_____
(4) _____ $_____

My TOTAL payroll deduction amount is: $_____

c. My monthly take-home pay is *(a. minus b.)*: . . . . . . . . . . . . . . . $_____

d. Other money I get each month is *(specify source and amount)*:

(1) _____ $_____
(2) _____ $_____

The TOTAL amount of other money is: $_____

e. **MY TOTAL MONTHLY INCOME IS** *(c. plus d.)*: . . . . . . . . . . . . . . . . . . . $_____

f. **The number of people in my family, including me, supported by this money is:** _____

7. a. ☐ I am *not* able to pay any of the court fees and costs.

b. ☐ I am able to pay *only* the following court fees and costs *(specify)*:

8. My monthly expenses are:

a. Rent or house payment & maintenance $_____
b. Food and household supplies . . . . . . $_____
c. Utilities and telephone . . . . . . . . . . $_____
d. Clothing . . . . . . . . . . . . . . . $_____
e. Laundry and cleaning . . . . . . . . . . . $_____
f. Medical and dental payments . . . . . . $_____
g. Insurance (life, health, accident, etc.) $_____
h. School, child care . . . . . . . . . . . . . $_____
i. Child, spousal support (prior marriage) $_____
j. Transportation and auto expenses (insurance, gas, repair) . . . . . . . . . . . $_____
k. Installment payments *(specify purpose and amount)*:

(1) _____ $_____
(2) _____ $_____
(3) _____ $_____

The TOTAL amount of monthly installment payments is: . . . . . . . . $_____

l. Amounts deducted due to wage assignments and earnings withholding orders $_____
m. Other expenses *(specify)*

(1) _____ _$_____
(2) _____ _$_____
(3) _____ $_____
(4) _____ $_____
(5) _____ $_____
(6) _____ $_____

The TOTAL amount of other monthly expenses is: . . . . . . . . . . . . . . . $_____

n. **MY TOTAL MONTHLY EXPENSES ARE** *(add a. through m.)*: . . . . . . . . . . . $_____

9. I own the following property:

a. Cash . . . . . . . . . . . . . . . . . . . . $_____
b. Checking, savings and credit union accounts *(list banks)*:

(1) _____ $_____
(2) _____ $_____
(3) _____ $_____

c. Cars, other vehicles and boat equity *(list make, year of each)*:

(1) _____ $_____
(2) _____ $_____
(3) _____ $_____

d. Real estate equity . . . . . . . . . . . . . $_____

e. Other personal property -- jewelry, furniture, furs, stocks, bonds, etc. *(list separately)*:

$_____

10. Other facts which support this application are *(describe unusual medical needs, expenses for recent family emergencies, or other unusual expenses to help the judge understand your budget)*. If more space is needed, attach page labeled attachment 10.

**WARNING: You must immediately tell the court if you become able to pay court fees or costs during this action. For the next three (3) years you may be ordered to appear in court and answer questions about your ability to pay court fees or costs.**

**APPLICATION FOR WAIVER OF COURT FEES AND COSTS**
(In Forma Pauperis)

| ATTORNEY OR PARTY WITHOUT ATTORNEY (Name and Address) | TELEPHONE NO. | FOR COURT USE ONLY |
|---|---|---|
| | | |

ATTORNEY FOR (Name)

NAME OF COURT, JUDICIAL DISTRICT OR BRANCH COURT, IF ANY

In the matter of the application of:

# ORDER ON APPLICATION FOR WAIVER OF COURT FEES AND COSTS

CASE NUMBER:

1. The application was filed
   a. on (date):
   b. by (name):
2. ☐ **IT IS ORDERED THAT the application is granted and the applicant is permitted to proceed in this action as follows:**
   a. ☐ without payment of any court fees or costs listed in rule 985(i), California Rules of Court.
   b. ☐ without payment of any court fees or costs listed in rule 985(i), California Rules of Court, except the following:

   c. ☐ without payment of the following court fees or costs (specify):

   d. The reasons for denial of any requested waiver are (specify):

   e. ☐ The clerk of the court is directed to mail a copy of this order to the applicant's attorney, if any, or to the applicant if unrepresented.
   f. ☐ All unpaid fees and costs shall be deemed to be taxable costs if applicant is entitled to costs and shall be a lien on any judgment recovered by the applicant and shall be paid to the clerk upon such recovery.
3. ☐ **IT IS ORDERED THAT the application is denied for the following reasons (specify):**

   a. **The applicant must pay any fees and costs due in this action within ten days from the date of service of this order or any paper filed by the applicant with the clerk will be of no effect.**
   b. The clerk of the court is directed to mail a copy of this order to all parties who have appeared in this action.
4. ☐ **IT IS ORDERED THAT a hearing be held.**
   a. The substantial evidentiary conflict to be resolved by the hearing is (specify):

   b. Applicant should be present at the hearing to be held:

| hearing date: | time: | in ☐ Dept.: | ☐ Div.: | ☐ Rm.: |
|---|---|---|---|---|
| address of court: | | | | |

   c. The clerk of the court is directed to mail a copy of this order to the applicant only.

Dated: . . . . . . . . . .                              _____

(Clerk's certification on page 2)                        (Signature of Judge)

Form Adopted by Rule 982
Judicial Council of California
Revised effective July 1, 1981

**ORDER ON APPLICATION FOR WAIVER OF COURT FEES AND COSTS (IN FORMA PAUPERIS)**

Govt. Code
§ 68511.3

| In the matter of the application of: | CASE NUMBER: |
|---|---|

## ORDER ON APPLICATION FOR WAIVER OF COURT FEES AND COSTS

### CLERK'S CERTIFICATE OF MAILING

I certify that I am not a party to this cause and that a copy of the foregoing was mailed first class, postage prepaid, in a sealed envelope addressed as shown below, and that the mailing and execution of the foregoing and execution of this certificate occurred at (place): . . . . . . . . . . . . . . . . . . . . . . . . . . . . . . . . California,

on (date): . . . . . . . . . . . . . . . . . . . . . . Clerk, by —————————————————
(Deputy)

### CLERK'S CERTIFICATION

(SEAL)

I certify that the foregoing is a true copy of the original on file in my office.

Dated: . . . . . . . . . . . . . . . . . . . . Clerk, by . . . . . . . . . . . . . . . . . . . .
(Deputy)

| PARTY WITHOUT AN ATTORNEY (*Name and Address*): | TELEPHONE NO.: | FOR COURT USE ONLY |
|---|---|---|

*In Pro Per*

**SUPERIOR COURT OF CALIFORNIA, COUNTY OF:**

STREET ADDRESS:

MAILING ADDRESS:

CITY AND ZIP CODE:

BRANCH NAME:

IN THE MATTER OF THE APPLICATION OF:

| **PROOF OF SERVICE (NAME CHANGE)** | CASE NUMBER: |
|---|---|

I declare that:

1. At the time of service I was at least 18 years of age and not a party to this legal action.

2. My business or residence address is: _____

   _____.

3. I served copies of the Order to Show Cause for Change of Name in the manner shown (*check either a or b below*):

   a. ☐ **Personal Service.** I personally delivered these papers to:

      (1) Name of person served: _____

      (2) Address where served: _____

                                _____

      (3) Date served: _____

      (4) Time served: _____

   b. ☐ **Certified mail, return receipt requested.** I deposited these papers in the United States mail, in a sealed envelope with postage fully prepaid. I used certified mail and requested a return receipt. The envelope was addressed and mailed to:

      (1) Name of person served: _____

      (2) Address to which documents were mailed: _____

                                _____

      (3) Date documents were mailed: _____

      (4) City and state where mailing occurred: _____

      (5) The signed return receipt is attached.

4. I declare under penalty of perjury under the laws of the State of California that the foregoing is true and correct.

Date:

.................................................

(Type or Print Name of Process Server)           Signature of Process Server

1
2
3
4
5
6
7
8
9
10
11
12
13
14
15
16
17
18
19
20
21
22
23
24
25
26
27
28

| ATTORNEY OR PARTY WITHOUT ATTORNEY *(Name and Address)*: | TELEPHONE NO.: | FOR COURT USE ONLY |
|---|---|---|

ATTORNEY FOR *(Name)*:

**SUPERIOR COURT OF CALIFORNIA, COUNTY OF**

STREET ADDRESS:

MAILING ADDRESS:

CITY AND ZIP CODE:

BRANCH NAME:

**MARRIAGE OF**

PETITIONER:

RESPONDENT:

| **EX PARTE APPLICATION FOR RESTORATION OF FORMER NAME AFTER ENTRY OF JUDGMENT AND ORDER** | CASE NUMBER: |
|---|---|

## APPLICATION

1. A judgment of dissolution or nullity was entered on *(date)*:

2. Applicant now requests that her former name be restored. Her former name is *(specify)*:

Date:

. . . . . . . . . . . . . . . . . . . . . . . . . . . . . . . . . . . . . . . . .        ▶

_____        _____
(TYPE OR PRINT NAME)                                            (SIGNATURE OF APPLICANT)

## ORDER

3. IT IS ORDERED that applicant's former name is restored to *(specify)*:

Date:

_____

☐ JUDGE OF THE SUPERIOR COURT     ☐ COMMISSIONER OF THE SUPERIOR COURT

[SEAL]

### CLERK'S CERTIFICATE

I certify that the foregoing is a true and correct copy of the original on file in my office.

Date: _____        Clerk, by _____ , Deputy

Form Adopted by Rule 1287.50
Judicial Council of California
1287.50 [New January 1, 1987]

**EX PARTE APPLICATION FOR RESTORATION OF FORMER NAME
AFTER ENTRY OF JUDGMENT AND ORDER**
(Family Law)

Civil Code, §§ 4362, 4457

# INDEX

# C A T A L O G
## ...more books from Nolo Press

## Estate Planning & Probate

### Plan Your Estate
*Attorney Denis Clifford. National 2nd ed.*
Covers every significant aspect of estate planning and gives detailed, specific instructions for preparing a living trust. Includes all the tear-out forms and step-by-step instructions to let you prepare an estate plan designed for your special needs. Good in all states except Louisiana.
$19.95/NEST

### Make Your Own Living Trust
*Attorney Denis Clifford. National 1st ed.*
Find out how a living trust works, how to create one, and how to determine what kind of trust is right for you. Contains all the forms and instructions you need to prepare a basic living trust to avoid probate, a marital life estate trust (A-B trust) to avoid probate and estate taxes, and a back-up will. Good in all states except Louisiana.
$19.95/LITR

### Nolo's Simple Will Book
*Attorney Denis Clifford. National 2nd ed.*
It's easy to write a legally valid will using this book. Includes all the instructions and sample forms you need to name a personal guardian for minor children, leave property to minor children or young adults and update a will when necessary. Good in all states except Louisiana.
$17.95/SWIL

### Who Will Handle Your Finances if You Can't?
*Attorneys Denis Clifford & Mary Randolph. National 1st ed.*
Give a trusted person legal authority to handle your financial matters if illness or old age makes it impossible for you to handle them yourself. Create a durable power of attorney for finances with the step-by-step instructions and fill-in-the-blank forms included in this book.
$19.95/FINA

### The Conservatorship Book
*Lisa Goldoftas & Attorney Carolyn Farren. California 1st ed.*
Provides forms and all instructions necessary to file conservatorship documents, appear in court, be appointed conservator and end a conservatorship.
$24.95/CNSV

### How to Probate an Estate
*Julia Nissley. California 7th ed.*
Save costly attorneys' fees by handling the probate process yourself. This book shows you step-by-step how to settle an estate. It also explains the simple procedures you can use to transfer assets that don't require probate. Forms included.
$34.95/PAE

## LAW FORM KITS

### Nolo's Law Form Kit: Wills
*Attorney Denis Clifford & Lisa Goldoftas. National 1st ed.*
All the forms and instructions you need to create a legally valid will, quickly and easily.
$14.95/KWL

## AUDIO CASSETTE TAPES

### Write Your Will
*Attorney Ralph Warner with Joanne Greene. National 1st ed. 60 minutes*
This tape answers the most frequently asked questions about writing a will and covers all key issues.
$14.95/TWYW

### 5 Ways to Avoid Probate
*Attorney Ralph Warner with Joanne Greene. National 1st ed. 60 minutes*
Provides clear, in-depth explanations of the principal probate avoidance techniques.
$14.95/TPRO

## SOFTWARE

 ### WillMaker®
*Version 5.0*

Make your own legal will and living will (healthcare directive)—and thoroughly document your final arrangements—with WillMaker 5. WillMaker's easy-to-use interview format takes you through each document step-by-step. On-line legal help is available throughout the program. Name a guardian for your children, make up to 100 property bequests, direct your healthcare in the event of coma or terminal illness, and let your loved ones know your wishes around your own final arrangements. Good in all states except Louisiana.
WINDOWS $69.95/WIW5
DOS $69.95/WI5
MACINTOSH $69.95/WM5

 ### Nolo's Personal RecordKeeper
*Version 3.0*
Finally, a safe, accessible place for your important records. Over 200 categories and subcategories to organize and store your important financial, legal and personal information, compute your net worth and create inventories for insurance records. Export your net worth and home inventory data to Quicken®.
DOS $49.95/FRI3
MACINTOSH $49.95/FRM3

 ### Nolo's Living Trust
*Version 1.0*

Put your assets into a trust and save your heirs the headache, time and expense of probate with this easy-to-use software. Use it to set up an individual or shared marital trust, transfer property to the trust, and change or revoke the trust at any time. Its manual guides you through the process, and legal help screens and an on-line glossary explain key legal terms and concepts. Good in all states except Louisiana.
MACINTOSH $79.95/LTM1

## Going to Court

### Represent Yourself in Court: How to Prepare & Try a Winning Case
*Attorneys Paul Bergman & Sara Berman-Barrett National 1st ed.*
Handle your own civil court case from start to finish without a lawyer with the most thorough guide to contested court cases ever published for the non-lawyer. Covers all aspects of civil trials including lining up persuasive witnesses, presenting testimony, cross-examining witnesses and even picking a jury.
$29.95/RYC

### Fight Your Ticket
*Attorney David Brown. California 5th ed.*
Shows you how to fight an unfair traffic ticket—when you're stopped, at arraignment, at trial and on appeal.
$18.95/FYT

### Everybody's Guide to Small Claims Court
*Attorney Ralph Warner.*
*National 5th ed.. California 11th ed.*
These books will help you decide if you should sue in Small Claims Court, show you how to file and serve papers, tell you what to bring to court and how to collect a judgment.
National $16.95/NSCC
California $16.95/CSCC

### Everybody's Guide to Municipal Court
*Judge Roderic Duncan. California 1st ed.*
Sue and defend cases for up to $25,000 in California Municipal Court. Step-by-step instructions for preparing and filing forms, gathering evidence and appearing in court.
$29.95/MUNI

### Collect Your Court Judgment
*Gini Graham Scott, Attorney Stephen Elias & Lisa Goldoftas. California 2nd ed.*
Contains step-by-step instructions and all the forms you need to collect a court judgment from the debtor's bank accounts, wages, business receipts, real estate or other assets.
$19.95/JUDG

### How to Change Your Name
*Attorneys David Loeb & David Brown. California 5th ed.*
All the forms and instructions you need to change your name in California.
$19.95/NAME

### The Criminal Records Book
*Attorney Warren Siegel. California 3rd ed.*
Shows you step-by-step how to seal criminal records, dismiss convictions, destroy marijuana records and reduce felony convictions.
$19.95/CRIM

### AUDIO CASSETTE TAPES

### Winning in Small Claims Court
*Attorney Ralph Warner with Joanne Greene.*
*National 1st ed. 60 minutes*
Strategies for preparing and presenting a winning small claims court case.
$14.95/TWIN

### Business/Workplace

### The Legal Guide for Starting & Running a Small Business
*Attorney Fred S. Steingold. National 1st ed.*
An essential resource for every small business owner. Find out how to form a sole proprietorship, partnership or corporation, negotiate a favorable lease, hire and fire employees, write contracts and resolve disputes.
$22.95/RUNS

### Sexual Harassment on the Job: What it is and How To Stop it.
*Attorneys William Petrocelli & Barbara Kate Repa.*
*National 1st ed.*
An invaluable resource for both employees experiencing harassment and employers interested in creating a policy against sexual harassment and a procedure for handling complaints.
$14.95/HARS

### Marketing Without Advertising
*Michael Phillips & Salli Rasberry. National 1st ed.*
Outlines practical steps for building and expanding a small business without spending a lot of money on advertising.
$14.00/MWAD

### Your Rights in the Workplace
*Barbara Kate Repa. National 2nd ed.*
The first comprehensive guide to workplace rights —from hiring to firing. Covers wages and overtime, parental leave, unemployment and disability insurance, worker's compensation, job safety, discrimination and illegal firings and layoffs.
$15.95/YRW

### How to Write a Business Plan
*Mike McKeever. National 4th ed.*
This book will show you how to write the business plan and loan package necessary to finance your business and make it work.
$19.95/SBS

### The Partnership Book
*Attorneys Denis Clifford & Ralph Warner.*
*National 4th ed.*
Shows you step-by-step how to write a solid partnership agreement that meets your needs. It covers initial contributions to the business, wages, profit-sharing, buyouts, death or retirement of a partner and disputes.
$24.95/PART

### Software Development: A Legal Guide
Book with Disk-DOS
*Attorney Stephen Fishman*
*National 1st ed.*
A reference bible for people in the software industry. This book explores the legal ins and outs of copyright, trade secret and patent protection, employment agreements, working with independent contractors and employees, development and publishing agreements and multimedia development. All contracts and agreements included on disk.
$44.95/SFT

### How to Form a Nonprofit Corporation
*Attorney Anthony Mancuso.*
*National 1st ed.*
Explains the legal formalities involved and provides detailed information on the differences in the law among all 50 states. It also contains forms for the Articles, Bylaws and Minutes you need, along with complete instructions for obtaining federal 501(c)(3) tax exemptions and qualifying for public charity status.
$24.95/NNP

### The California Nonprofit Corporation Handbook
*Attorney Anthony Mancuso.*
*California 6th ed.*
Shows you step-by-step how to form and operate a nonprofit corporation in California. It includes the latest corporate and tax law changes, and the forms for the Articles, Bylaws and Minutes.
$29.95/NON

### How to Form Your Own Corporation
*Attorney Anthony Mancuso*
*California 7th ed.. New York 2nd ed..*
*Texas 4th ed.. Florida 3rd ed.*
These books contain the forms, instructions and tax information you need to incorporate a small business yourself and save hundreds of dollars in lawyers' fees.
California $29.95/CCOR
New York $24.95/NYCO
Texas $29.95/TCOR
*How to Form Your Own Corporation* is also available with incorporation forms on disk for these states:
New York 1st ed. DOS $39.95/NYCI,
                MACINTOSH $39.95/NYCM
Texas 4th ed. DOS $39.95/TCI
Florida 3rd ed. DOS $39.95/FCCO

### The California Professional Corporation Handbook
*Attorney Anthony Mancuso.*
*California 5th ed.*
Health care professionals, lawyers, accountants and members of certain other professions must fulfill special requirements when forming a corporation in California. Contains up-to-date tax information plus all the forms and instructions necessary.
$34.95/PROF

### The Independent Paralegal's Handbook
*Attorney Ralph Warner.*
*National 2nd ed.*
Provides legal and business guidelines for anyone who wants to go into business as an independent paralegal helping consumers with routine legal tasks.
$24.95 PARA

### Getting Started as an Independent Paralegal
*Attorney Ralph Warner. National 2nd ed.*
*Two tapes, approximately 2 hours*
Practical and legal advice on going into business as an independent paralegal from the author of *The Independent Paralegal's Handbook*.
$44.95/GSIP

### How to Start Your Own Business: Small Business Law
*Attorney Ralph Warner with Joanne Greene. National 1st ed. 60 minutes*
What every small business owner needs to know about organizing as a sole proprietorship, partnership or corporation, protecting the business name, renting space, hiring employees and paying taxes.
$14.95/TBUS

### Nolo's Partnership Maker
*Version 1.0*
*Attorney Tony Mancuso & Michael Radtke*
Prepare a legal partnership agreement for doing business in any state. Select and assemble the standard partnership clauses provided or create your own customized agreement. Includes on-line legal help screens, glossary and tutorial, and a manual that takes you through the process step-by-step.
DOS   $129.95/PAGI1

### California Incorporator
*Version 1.0 (good only in CA)*
*Attorney Tony Mancuso*
Answer the questions on the screen and this software program will print out the 35-40 pages of documents you need to make your California corporation legal. A 200-page manual explains the incorporation process.
DOS   $129.00/INCI

## The Neighborhood

### Neighbor Law: Fences, Trees, Boundaries & Noise
*Attorney Cora Jordan. National 1st ed.*
Answers common questions about the subjects that most often trigger disputes between neighbors: fences, trees, boundaries and noise. It explains how to find the law and resolve disputes without a nasty lawsuit.
$14.95/NEI

### Safe Homes, Safe Neighborhoods: Stopping Crime Where You Live
*Stephanie Mann with M.C. Blakeman. National 1st ed.*
Learn how you and your neighbors can work together to protect yourselves, your families and property from crime. Explains how to form a neighborhood crime prevention group; avoid burglaries, muggings and rapes; combat gangs and drug dealing; improve home security and make the neighborhood safer for children.
$14.95/SAFE

### Dog Law
*Attorney Mary Randolph. National 1st ed.*
A practical guide to the laws that affect dog owners and their neighbors. Answers common questions about biting, barking, veterinarians and more.
$12.95/DOG

## Money Matters

### Stand Up to the IRS
*Attorney Fred Daily. National 2nd ed.*
Gives detailed strategies on surviving an audit, appealing an audit decision, going to Tax Court and dealing with IRS collectors. It also discusses filing delinquent tax returns, tax crimes, concerns of small business people and getting help from the IRS ombudsman.
$21.95/SIRS

### How to File for Bankruptcy
*Attorneys Stephen Elias, Albin Renauer & Robin Leonard. National 4th ed.*
Trying to decide whether or not filing for bankruptcy makes sense? This book contains an overview of the process and all the forms plus step-by-step instructions you need to file for Chapter 7 Bankruptcy.
$25.95/HFB

### Money Troubles: Legal Strategies to Cope with Your Debts
*Attorney Robin Leonard. National 2nd ed.*
Essential for anyone who has gotten behind on bills. It shows how to obtain a credit file, negotiate with persistent creditors, challenge wage attachments, contend with repossessions and more.
$16.95/MT

### Simple Contracts for Personal Use
*Attorney Stephen Elias & Marcia Stewart. National 2nd ed.*
Contains clearly written legal form contracts to buy and sell property, borrow and lend money, store and lend personal property, release others from personal liability, or pay a contractor to do home repairs. Includes agreements to arrange child care and other household help.
$16.95/CONT

### Nolo's Law Form Kit: Personal Bankruptcy
*Attorneys Steve Elias, Albin Renauer & Robin Leonard and Lisa Goldoftas. National 1st ed.*
All the forms and instructions you need to file for Chapter 7 bankruptcy.
$14.95/KBNK

### Nolo's Law Forms Kit: Rebuild Your Credit
*Attorney Robin Leonard. National 1st ed.*
Provides strategies for dealing with debts and rebuilding your credit. Shows you how to negotiate with creditors and collection agencies, clean up your credit file, devise a spending plan and get credit in your name.
$14.95/KCRD

### Nolo's Law Form Kit: Power of Attorney
*Attorneys Denis Clifford & Mary Randolph and Lisa Goldoftas. National 1st ed.*
Create a conventional power of attorney to assign someone you trust to take of your finances, business, real estate or children when you are away or unavailable. Provides all the forms with step-by-step instructions.
$14.95/KPA

### Nolo's Law Form Kit: Loan Agreements
*Attorney Stephen Elias, Marcia Stewart & Lisa Goldoftas. National 1st ed.*
Provides all the forms and instructions necessary to create a legal and effective promissory note. Shows how to decide on an interest rate, set a payment schedule and keep track of payments.
$14.95/KLOAN

### Nolo's Law Form Kit: Buy and Sell Contracts
*Attorney Stephen Elias, Marcia Stewart & Lisa Goldoftas. National 1st ed.*
Step-by-step instructions and all the forms necessary for creating bills of sale for cars, boats, computers, electronic equipment, and other personal property.
$9.95/K CONT

## Family Matters

### Nolo's Pocket Guide to Family Law
*Attorneys Robin Leonard & Stephen Elias. Nat, 3rd ed.*
Here's help for anyone who has a question or problem involving family law— marriage, divorce, adoption or living together.
$14.95/FLD

## Divorce & Money

*Violet Woodhouse & Victoria Felton-Collins
with M.C. Blakeman.
National 2nd ed.*
Explains how to evaluate such major assets as family homes and businesses, investments, pensions, and how to arrive at a division of property that is fair to both sides.
$21.95/DIMO

## The Living Together Kit

*Attorneys Toni Ihara & Ralph Warner. National 6th ed.*
A detailed guide designed to help the increasing number of unmarried couples living together understand the laws that affect them. Sample agreements and instructions are included.
$17.95/LTK

## A Legal Guide for Lesbian and Gay Couples

*Attorneys Hayden Curry, Denis Clifford & Robin Leonard. National 7th ed.*
This book shows lesbian and gay couples how to write a living-together contract, plan for medical emergencies, understand the practical and legal aspects of having and raising children and plan their estates. Includes forms and sample agreements.
$21.95/LG

## California Marriage & Divorce Law

*Attorneys Ralph Warner,
Toni Ihara & Stephen Elias. California 11th ed.*
Explains community property, pre-nuptial contracts, foreign marriages, buying a house, getting a divorce, dividing property, and more. Pre-nuptial contracts included.
$19.95/MARR

## Divorce: A New Yorker's Guide to Doing it Yourself

*Bliss Alexandra. New York 1st ed.*
Step-by-step instructions and all the forms you need to do your own divorce and save thousands of dollars in legal fees. Shows you how to divide property, arrange custody of the children, set child support and maintenance (alimony), draft a divorce agreement and fill out and file all forms.
$24.95/NYDIV

## How to Raise or Lower Child Support in California

*Judge Roderic Duncan & Attorney Warren Siegal. California 1st ed.*
Appropriate for parents on either side of the support issue. All the forms and instructions necessary to raise or lower an existing child support order.
$16.95/CHLD

## The Guardianship Book

*Lisa Goldoftas & Attorney David Brown. California 1st ed.*
Provides step-by-step instructions and the forms needed to obtain a legal guardianship of a minor without a lawyer.
$19.95/GB

## How to Do Your Own Divorce

*Attorney Charles Sherman
(Texas ed. by Sherman & Simons)
California 19th ed. & Texas 5th ed.*
These books contain all the forms and instructions you need to do your own uncontested divorce without a lawyer.
California $21,95/CDIV
Texas $17.95/TDIV

## Practical Divorce Solutions

*Attorney Charles Sherman.
California 2nd ed.*
Covers the emotional aspects of divorce and provides an overview of the legal and financial considerations.
$12.95/PDS

## How to Adopt Your Stepchild in California

*Frank Zagone & Attorney Mary Randolph.
California 4th ed.*
Provides sample forms and step-by-step instructions for completing a simple uncontested stepparent adoption in California.
$22.95/ADOP

# Patent, Copyright & Trademark

## Trademark: How to Name Your Business & Product

*Attorneys Kate McGrath & Stephen Elias, With Trademark Attorney Sarah Shena. National 1st ed.*
Learn how to choose a name or logo that others can't copy, conduct a trademark search, register a trademark with the U.S. Patent and Trademark Office and protect and maintain the trademark.
$29.95/TRD

## Patent It Yourself

*Attorney David Pressman.
National 3rd ed.*
From the patent search to the actual application, this book covers everything including the use and licensing of patents, successful marketing and how to deal with infringement.
$36.95/PAT

## The Inventor's Notebook

*Fred Grissom & Attorney David Pressman.
National 1st ed.*
Helps you document the process of successful independent inventing by providing forms, instructions, references to relevant areas of patent law, a bibliography of legal and non-legal aids and more.
$19.95/INOT

## The Copyright Handbook

*Attorney Stephen Fishman.
National 1st ed.*
Provides forms and step-by-step instructions for protecting all types of written expression under U.S. and international copyright law. Covers copyright infringement, fair use, works for hire and transfers of copyright ownership.
$24.95/COHA

# Landlords & Tenants

## The Landlord's Law Book, Vol. 1: Rights & Responsibilities

*Attorneys David Brown & Ralph Warner.
California 4th ed.*
Essential for every California landlord. Covers deposits, leases and rental agreements, inspections (tenants' privacy rights), habitability (rent withholding), ending a tenancy, liability and rent control. Forms included.
$32.95/LBRT

## The Landlord's Law Book, Vol. 2: Evictions

*Attorney David Brown. California 4th ed.*
Shows step-by-step how to go to court and evict a tenant. Contains all the tear-out forms and necessary instructions.
$32.95/LBEV

## Tenants' Rights

*Attorneys Myron Moskovitz & Ralph Warner.
California 11th ed.*
This practical guide to dealing with your landlord explains your rights under federal law, California law and rent control ordinances. Forms included.
$15.95/CTEN

# Homeowners

## How to Buy a House in California

*Attorney Ralph Warner, Ira Serkes & George Devine.
California 2nd ed.*
Effective strategies for finding a house, working with a real estate agent, making an offer and negotiating intelligently. Includes information on all types of mortgages as well as private financing options.
$19.95/BHCA

## For Sale By Owner

*George Devine. California 2nd ed.*
Everything you need to know to sell your own house, from pricing and marketing, to writing a contract and going through escrow. Disclosure and contract forms included.
$24.95/FSBO

### Homestead Your House

*Attorneys Ralph Warner,*
*Charles Sherman & Toni Ihara. California 8th ed.*
Shows you how to file a Declaration of
Homestead and includes complete
instructions and tear-out forms.
$9.95/HOME

### The Deeds Book

*Attorney Mary Randolph.*
*California 2nd ed.*
Shows you how to fill out and file the right
kind of deed when transferring property.
Outlines the legal requirements of real
property transfer.
$15.95/DEED

### LAW FORM KITS

### Nolo's Law form Kit: Leases & Rental Agreements

*Attorney Ralph Warner & Marcia Stewart*
*California 1st ed.*
With these easy-to-use forms and
instructions, California landlords can
prepare their own rental application, fixed
term lease and month -to-month rental
agreement.
$14.95/KLEAS

## Just For Fun

### Devil's Advocates: The Unnatural History of Lawyers

*by Andrew & Jonathan Roth. National 1st ed.*
A hilarious look at the history of the legal
profession.
$12.95/DA

### 29 Reasons Not to Go to Law School

*Attorneys Ralph Warner & Toni Ihara. National 3rd ed.*
Filled with humor, this book can save you
three years, $70,000 and your sanity.
$9.95/29R

### Poetic Justice: The Funniest, Meanest Things Ever Said About Lawyers

*Edited by Jonathan & Andrew Roth. National 1st ed.*
A great gift for anyone in the legal
profession who has managed to maintain a
sense of humor.
$8.95/PJ

### Nolo's Favorite Lawyer Jokes on Disk

Over 200 jokes and hilariously nasty
remarks about lawyers. 100% guaranteed
to produce an evening of chuckles and
drive every lawyer you know nuts.
DOS 3-1/2  $9.95/JODI
MACINTOSH  $9.95/JODM

## Older Americans

### Beat the Nursing Home Trap: A Consumer's Guide to Choosing and Financing Long-Term Care (formerly Elder Care)

*Joseph Matthews. National 2nd ed.*
This practical guide shows how to protect
assets, arrange home health care, find
nursing and non-nursing home residences,
evaluate nursing home insurance and
understand Medicare, Medicaid and other
benefit programs.
$18.95/ELD

### Social Security, Medicare & Pensions

*Attorney Joseph Matthews with Dorothy Matthews*
*Berman. National 5th ed.*
Offers invaluable guidance through the
current maze of rights and benefits for
those 55 and over, including Medicare,
Medicaid and Social Security retirement
and disability benefits, and age
discrimination protections.
$15.95/SOA

## Research & Reference

### Legal Research: How to Find and Understand the Law

*Attorneys Stephen Elias & Susan Levinkind.*
*National 3rd ed.*
A valuable tool on its own or as a
companion to just about every other Nolo
book. Gives easy-to-use, step-by-step
instructions on how to find legal
information.
$19.95/LRES

### Legal Research Made Easy: A Roadmap Through the Law Library Maze

*2-1/2 hr. videotape and 40-page manual*
*Nolo Press/Legal Star Communications. National 1st ed.*
Professor Bob Berring explains how to use
all the basic legal research tools in your
local law library with an easy-to-follow six-
step research plan and a sense of humor.
$89.95/LRME

## Consumer

### Nolo's Pocket Guide to California Law

*Attorney Lisa Guerin & Nolo Press Editors.*
*California 2nd ed.*
Get quick clear answers to questions about
child support, custody, consumer rights,
employee rights, government benefits,
divorce, bankruptcy, adoption, wills and
much more.
$10.95/CLAW

### Nolo's Pocket Guide to Consumer Rights

*Barbara Kaufman.*
*California 2nd ed.*
Practical advice on hundreds of consumer
topics. Shows Californians how and where
to complain about everything from
accountants, misleading advertisements
and lost baggage to vacation scams and
dishonored warranties.
$14.95/CAG

### Legal Breakdown: 40 Ways to Fix Our Legal System

*Nolo Press Editors & Staff.*
*National 1st ed.*
Forty common-sense proposals to make
our legal system fairer, faster, cheaper and
more accessible.
$8.95/LEG

### How to Win Your Personal Injury Claim

*Attorney Joseph Matthews. National 1st ed.*
Armed with the right information anyone
can handle a personal injury claim. This
step-by-step guide shows you how to avoid
insurance company run-arounds, evaluate
what your claim is worth, obtain a full and
fair settlement and save for yourself what
you would pay a lawyer.
$24.95/PICL

### LAW FORM KITS

### Nolo's Law Form Kit: Hiring Child Care & Household Help

*Attorney Barbara Kate Repa & Lisa Goldoftas*
*National 1st ed.*
All the necessary forms and instructions
for fulfilling your legal and tax
responsibilities. Includes employment
contracts, applications forms and required
IRS forms.
$14.95/KCHLD

## Immigration

### How to Get a Green Card: Legal Ways to Stay in the U.S.A.

*Attorney Loida Nicolas Lewis with Len T. Madlanscay.*
*National 1st ed.*
Written by a former INS attorney, this
book clearly explains the steps involved in
getting a green card. It covers who can
qualify, what documents to present, and
how to fill out all the forms and have them
processed. Tear-out forms included.
$19.95/GRN

# order form

| CODE | QUANTITY | ITEM | UNIT PRICE | TOTAL |
|------|----------|------|------------|-------|
| | | | | |
| | | | | |
| | | | | |
| | | | | |
| | | | | |
| | | | Subtotal | |
| | | | California residents add Sales Tax | |
| | | Shipping & Handling ($4 for 1 item; $5 for 2-3 items; +$.50 each additional item) | | |
| | | 2nd day UPS (additional $5; $8 in Alaska & Hawaii) | | |
| | | | **T O T A L** | |

Name

Address (UPS to street address; Priority Mail to P.O. boxes)

**METHOD OF PAYMENT**

☐ Check enclosed   ☐ VISA   ☐ Mastercard   ☐ Discover Card   ☐ American Express

Account #                                          Expiration Date

Authorizing Signature                              Daytime Phone

**Send to**

NOLO PRESS, 950 PARKER STREET, BERKELEY, CA 94710
Allow 2-3 weeks for delivery. PRICES SUBJECT TO CHANGE.

# visit our store in Berkeley

If you live in the Bay Area, be sure to visit the Nolo Press Bookstore
on the corner of 9th & Parker Streets in west Berkeley. You'll find
our complete line of books and software—all at a discount.

Call 1-510-704-2248 for hours.

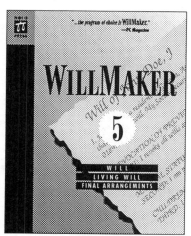

# Get 25% Off Your Next Purchase

# FREE NOLO NEWS SUBSCRIPTION

When you register, we'll send you our quarterly newspaper, the *Nolo News,* free for two years. (U.S. addresses only.) Here's what you'll get in every issue:

## INFORMATIVE ARTICLES

Written by Nolo editors, articles provide practical legal information on issues you encounter in everyday life: family law, wills, debts, consumer rights, and much more.

## UPDATE SERVICE

The *Nolo News* keeps you informed of legal changes that affect any Nolo book and software program.

## BOOK AND SOFTWARE REVIEWS

We're always looking for good legal and consumer books and software from other publishers. When we find them, we review them and offer them in our mail order catalog.

## ANSWERS TO YOUR LEGAL QUESTIONS

Our readers are always challenging us with good questions on a variety of legal issues. So in each issue, "Auntie Nolo" gives sage advice and sound information.

## COMPLETE NOLO PRESS CATALOG

The *Nolo News* contains an up-to-the-minute catalog of all Nolo books and software, which you can order using our toll-free "800" order line. And you can see at a glance if you're using an out-of-date version of a Nolo product.

## LAWYER JOKES

Nolo's famous lawyer joke column continually gets the goat of the legal establishment. If we print a joke you send in, you'll get a $20 Nolo gift certificate.

**We promise *never* to give your name and address to any other organization.**

---

**Your Registration Card**

**Complete and Mail Today**

**HOW TO CHANGE YOUR NAME**                                          **Registration Card**

We'd like to know what you think! Please take a moment to fill out and return this postage paid card for a free two-year subscription to the *Nolo News.* If you already receive the *Nolo News,* we'll extend your subscription.

Name _____ Ph.( ) _____

Address _____

City _____ State _____ Zip _____

Where did you hear about this book? _____

For what purpose did you use this book? _____

| Did you consult a lawyer? | | Yes | No | | Not Applicable | | |
|---|---|---|---|---|---|---|---|
| Was it easy for you to use this book? | (very easy) | 5 | 4 | 3 | 2 | 1 | (very difficult) |
| Did you find this book helpful? | (very) | 5 | 4 | 3 | 2 | 1 | (not at all) |

Comments _____

_____

_____

_____

_____

_____

THANK YOU                                                              **NAME 6.0**

NO POSTAGE
NECESSARY
IF MAILED
IN THE
UNITED STATES

**BUSINESS REPLY MAIL**
FIRST-CLASS MAIL PERMIT NO 3283 BERKELEY CA

POSTAGE WILL BE PAID BY ADDRESSEE

**NOLO PRESS**
**950 Parker Street**
**Berkeley CA 94710-9867**